e-Library

Dr. C.K. Sharma
Sushma Gupta
Anil Kumar

SHREE PUBLISHERS & DISTRIBUTORS
NEW DELHI-110 002

Edition : 2010

Published by :
SHREE PUBLISHERS & DISTRIBUTORS
22/4735 Prakash Deep, Ansari Road,
Darya Ganj, New Delhi–110 002

ISBN : 978-81–8329–373–0

Printed by :
Tarun Offset
Delhi–110 053

e-Library

DEDICATED

to

Dr. M.K. Jain

a man of vision, learning,

hardwork and always

a 'pillar of strength' to others.

Preface

e-Learning means learning through electronic sources or medias. The present generation is taking interest in e-Learning sources than the traditional sources. This has caused the establishment of e-Libraries in various institutions, but it has not taken the due recognition till today in the countries like India being insufficient facilities and funding. e-Libraries are functioning in European countries since 1991. However Indian Universities, major Science and Technical Institutes and Corporates have adopted these modern techniques and also making efforts if not accepted it.

e-Library is fifth generation library and going ahead with new millennium generation which provide video facilities and face to face deliverations on communication channels through internet. Modern libraries adopted interactive use of ICT to facilitate learning and systems consists of access tools viz. searching, retrieval locating documents, browsing, Navigation, archiving digital documents, content delivery, digital preservation, inducing, presentation, extraction, distribution, elicitation, editing, interfacing, online and soon.

There are various operation tools of e-Library as e-Mail, mailing lists, news groups, bulletins board, web form, polling, instant messaging, chat, conferencing, internet telephony, video conferencing and virtual world etc.

However, e-Library provides e-Learning facilities to its clientes with its modern techniques, and appliances. e-Library has been taken a shape and designed in many universities and institutes in India.

e-Library is a book of our efforts made out of constant learning and readings of many books, articles and also papers presented in seminars. We cannot ignore the literature and their authors whose ideas have been taken into consideration in this book. We pay our gratitude to all such authors and their creations.

— C.K. Sharma
— Sushma Gupta
— Anil Kumar

Contents

	Preface	*(vii)*
1.	**Introduction**	**1**
	Library and e-Learning	1
	Objectives	2
	Functions	2
	Convergence	2
	Technical inter Operability and System Components	3
	Space Environment	5
	Complexities and Interactions	5
	Digital Rights Management	7
	Portals	8
	Authority	9
2.	**Libraries and Growth of e-Learning**	**11**
	OCLC Programmes	12
	Learning Methodologies and Technology	12
	Metadata and Repositories	12
	Training	13
	Collaboration	13
	e-Learning and Libraries	13
	E-learning in Distance Education	13
	Course Management System	14
	Effective Policy	17
	Metadata Strategies	18
	Integration of Library and Learning Management Systems Environments	20
	Functional Requirement	20
	Cultural Requirement	21

Content Management 21
Technical Infrastructure 22
Training 22
Standards 22
Strategies 23
Collaborative Opportunities 23
Integrating Library Services 24
Digital Asset Repositories 24

3. e-Learning and e-Learners 26
E-learning 26
Principles of e-Learning 26
Quality 27
Equity 27
Information Literacy 27
Integration 28
Communication 28
Whole-process Coating 28
Plan 29
Quality Assurance Framework 29
Printed and Electronic Articles 30
CD ROMs or DVDs 31
Multimedia 31
Electronic Resources 31
Network Access for e-Learners, Capacity and Bandwidth 31
Access to and Location of Resources 32
Document Delivery 32
Access to a Local Library and Informaiton Service 33
Access to Help and Advice 33
Information Literacy 33
Integration 34
Communication 35
Process Costing 36

U.K Libraries 37

4. e-Learning—A Synchronous and Synchronous Tools **40**

Content Creation 41

Administration 42

The Benefits and Limitations of e-Learning 42

5. e-Libray : Learning Environment and Teaching Development **44**

Information Technology Update 44

Changing Paradigm for Schools 45

Information and Communication Technology 47

Global Gateway to Online Resources for Teacher Development 48

Multimedia Educational Resources for Learning and Online Teaching and e-Library 50

I-SITe (Information SITE) 50

Knowledge Resources 51

Web Portals 51

Virtual Library 52

National Grid for Learning 52

e-Learning and Teacher Development 53

6. e-Library for the Knowledge Society **54**

e-Learning and Students 55

Fundamentals 56

EdNA Online 58

Features 59

Functions 59

7. e-Learning—A Financial Study **62**

Saving on Overhead 64

Faculty Concerns About Course Development 64

Possible Solutions 66

Virtual University 66

Brick-and-Mortar Versus Blended Learning 67

Costly 68

8. e- Learning and e-Library **69**
e-Learning 69
Virtual Learning 70
e-Learning Tools 73
Indian Scene 74
e-Learning as a Media 77
Impart of e-Learning 79
e-Learning Framework 79
Intiative Efforts for e-Learning 82
Features of e-Learning 93
Successful Implementation of e-Learning 85
Digital Libraries 85
Metadata 89
Operational Tools for Digital Library 89
Staffing and Training 89
Material Stored 90
Wrapper Software 91
Interface 91
Push Service 92
e-Learning 94
Intelligent Search 94
Visualization of Search Results 95
Conceptual Searching 95
9. Digital Collection and e-Learning **98**
Evaluation of Digital Collection 98
Definition 98
Objectives 99
Components 99
e-Learning and the Campus 100
Prospects 100
Instructional Models for Using Weblogs in e-Learning 101
The Hybrid Experience 102
The Blog 102

	Data Type and Format	102
	Components of Digital Material	104
	Type of Material	105
	Type of File Format	106
	Operating System	108
	Steps in Preservation Process	109
10.	**e-Book and e-Library**	**111**
	The Evolution of the Page and Book	112
	Publisher	112
	e-Content-vs-e-Learning	113
	Contents	114
	Software Standards	115
	Hardware Standards	116
	Digital Rights Management	116
	Access	117
	Archiving and Long Term Access	118
	The Market and Pricing	118
	Academic Institution and e-Book	119
	Print Media Journal	120
	Inquiry Based Learning	121
11.	**Electronic Publishing**	**125**
	ACJ Net	125
	Definitions	125
	Grolier's Electronic Encyclopedia	126
	Issues in Electronic Publishing	127
	Designing e-Documents for WWW	127
	e-Publishing and Communications	128
	Media Type and File Format	129
	New Publishing Paradigm	134
	Other e-Repositories	136
	Publishers and Titles	137
	INFLIBNET Initiative	139

12.	**e-Journal**	**142**
	Electronic Journal of Academic and Special Libraries	143
	Basic Steps	144
	Survival	145
	Library Image	145
	Total Quality Managment	146
	Total Quality Management : Importance	148
	Factors	149
13.	**e-Writing**	**150**
	The Impact on Computers on Traditional Writings	152
	Fixity to Fluidity	154
14.	**e-Literature**	**157**
	Project Gutenberg	158
	Mission	158
	Consideration for every individual	159
15.	**e-Learning in Distance Education**	**160**
	Significance of Distant Education	160
	Distance Education	161
	Electronic Media Use in Distant Education	162
	The Internet and Distance Education	163
	Limitations of e-Learning	165
16.	**e-Resources**	**167**
	Open Sources	168
	Full Text Databases	169
	Gateway	171
	Important Gateway	173
	Approach to e-Learning	173
	e-Learning and e-Society	174
	Library Consortium	174
	Problems of Designing Hypermedia	175
	Components	176
	Hypermedia in Learning	176

17.	**Modern Learning Centers and e-Learning**	**177**
	Knowledge Representation	177
	Words and Thesaurus	178
	Knowledge Structures	179
	Hypertext	181
	Links with User	185
	Documents	176
18.	**Computer Networks**	**189**
	Information on the Network	194
	Grid Computing	196
	e-Book	197
	Computer Connectivity	199
	User Needs	201
	Access for Learning	203
	Library Materials	206
19.	**Development of Libraries and Learning Centers in the Development of Learning and Thinking in Ancient and Medieval India**	**207**
	Development of Libraries and Learning Centers	207
	Education System	209
	Centers of Learning	209
	Takshashila and Other Libraries	210
	Hindu Kings – Royal Libraries	211
	Bibliography	**213**

1
Introduction

Libraries and E-Learning

For the last decade, universities have been grappling with the growing complexities arising out of the pervasive influence of information and communication technologies. The growing interdependence of the various system environments led to a focus on organizational restructuring as a solution to a range of political and functional problems. Towards the end of the decade, it become apparent that organizational restructuring its not complete in itself but IT services, management information systems and (sometimes) flexible learning centres has also not necessarily lead to better service outcomes. Librarians, IT personnel and those leading the teaching and learning support services, still have very different world views of the means by which services should be organized. Underlying this ongoing cultural and professional struggle are four key concepts, such as:

(a) the nature of the learning experience,

(b) service convergence,

(c) intero-perability and

(d) sustainability.

For the learning experience to be derived from online environment, it was to be expected that the sheer struggle of implementing learning management systems, and in getting academic staff to use them, would temporarily overshadow concerns about the quality of the learning experience. The present generation of learning management systems are limited in functionality, however, they have facilitated a wide and varied range of online interaction in the teaching area. As a broad generalization, academic staff have mainly automated existing practices very much within the boundaries of traditional classroom practices.

Objectives of E-learning

- To ensure that access to high quality information is integrated into course provision.
- To equip e-Learners with the information skills to exploit that information.
- To provide appropriate advice and assistance to e-Learners in information searching.
- To address the related communications and costing issues.

Functions of e-Learning

1. Transformation to learning-centred communities, which can be achieved with learning-centred technology.
2. Faculty development transitioning to learning-centred technology.
3. Transformational faculty development must be coupled to institutional change.
4. Course-management systems will be a critical enabling force driving the institutional change.

Service Convergence

There are two kinds of convergence:

(a) Structural convergence

(b) Service convergence

There is a fundamental difference between organizational structural convergence and service convergence. Structural convergence is driven by the providers of service, whereas service convergence begins with user needs. In view of the facilities and success of student and the faculty in an online learning and information environment, the coupling of learning and information is quite deliberate because no online learning environment can be successful without relatively seamless access to information resources at the point of need.

Technical Interoperability and Systems Components

It is a need for service convergence in the emerging online learning and information environments. The technical capability supporting the so-called "learning space" is evolving with considerable speed and the interaction of traditional library systems with this systems component framework needs careful attention. Almost all universities now have one or more learning management systems which handle the administration and delivery of units of study with varying degrees of complexity. To date, they have been fairly close systems. Over the past three years, content management systems have been introduced, primarily as a means of controlling website development. The explosive growth of the web has been matched by a huge effort within institutions to develop websites as a "window" to particular sets of information.

According to Browning and Lowndes "A Content Management System (CMS) is a concept rather than a product. It is a concept that embraces a set of processes. Institutional needs are often highly individual (reflecting the heterogeneity of their processes and back-end systems) and so the task of implementing a Content Management System will inevitably contain significant components according to the need of the custoures."

There are many other systems but they are "Substantial overlaps with documents management systems, knowledge management systems, enterprise application integration systems, e-commerce systems and portals. The potentially all embracing of the Content Management System environment invokes "turf-wars" and the organizational implications of maintaining such a controlled environment are yet to be understood.

Learning Content Managements Systems (LCMS's) have emerged as a means of managing repositories of learning objects. The most significant aspect of this latest development is the separation of course management and learning content. The positioning of LCMS's in the learning space remains a very contentious issue because little is understood of how such systems should interact with an Learning Management System and the resultant traffic management problems remain as a major challenge.

In modern age online services and infrastructure have been added to traditional services and infrastructure puts great pressure on all parts of the institution. For some time, libraries and IT services have been competing vigorously for resources and there is now enormous demand from faculty members for resources to boost online learning infrastructure. Therefore, sustainability is a key issue and long-term sustainability is unlikely without a realignment of business goals and a transformation of organizational and learning practices.

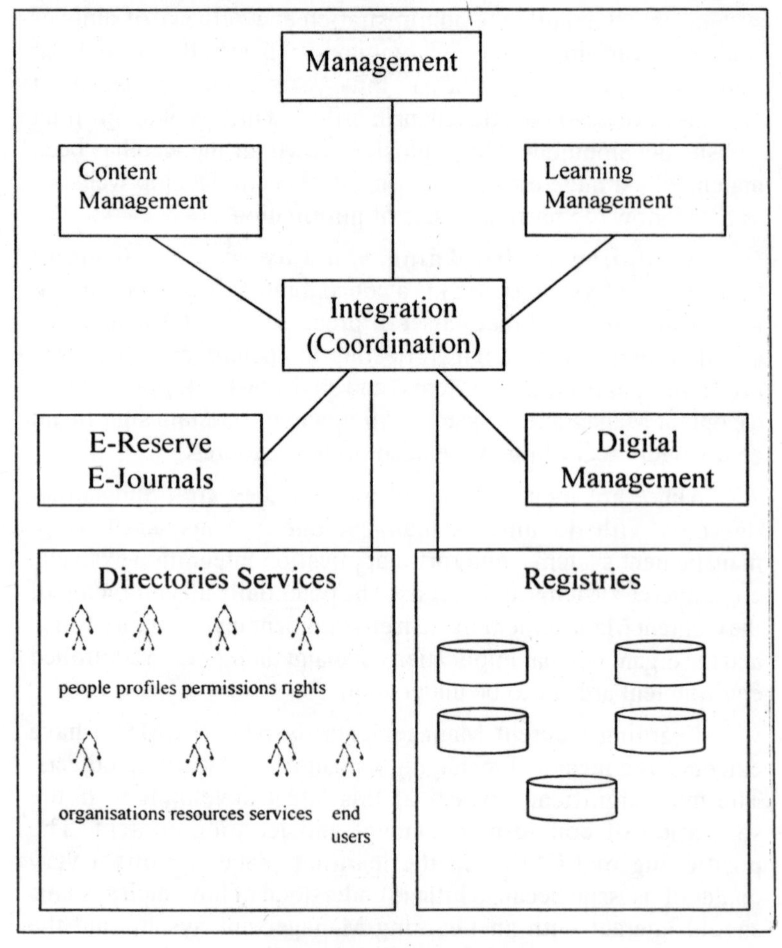

Functional view points

Libraries are particularly found their position difficult to find an adequate balance between the print and online information resource requirements. They face a further threat if they are unable to find a role in the online learning space which is relevant.

Space Environment

There are a number of "chunks" which make up the learning and information space in the online environment. COLIS has depicted the functional "chunks" in the learning and information space as shown below:

Complexities and Interactions

The complexities of the interactions required to make this learning and information space "come-to-life" or life serving are most challenging.

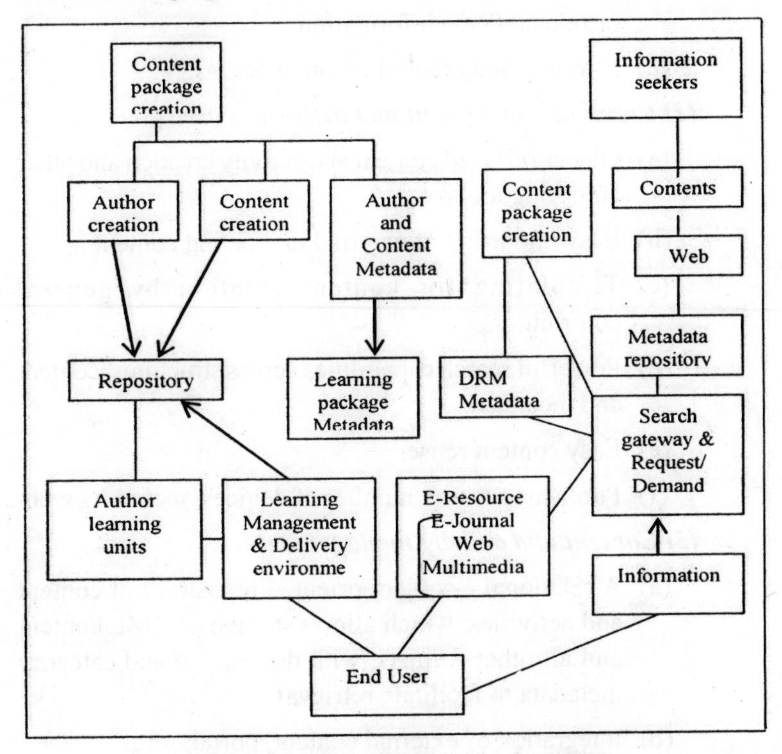

Interaction Complexities of e-Learning

Information Model

While formulating the information model, we may categorise the challenges as under:

(1) User based Challanges-

(a) Portal-based access to a variety of contents, activities, communities and tools, based on user profile.

(b) Powerful search capabilities across structure, content and metadata.

(c) Dynamic delivery/ access to specific content, activities and communities based on profiles, assessment or other data or queries.

(d) User-configurable pro-active agents which monitor sources and repositories to automatically alert users or relevant new information.

(e) Wireless and other alternative access.

(2) Creation and content and activities based

(a) Object-oriented content and activity creation and other authoring tools.

(b) Easy importing of external or existing content.

(c) Templating for content creation by general contributors.

(d) Powerful search capabilities across structures, content and metadata

(e) Easy content reuse.

(f) Publishing to any number of devices, including web.

(3) Content and activity management

(a) A relational or object-oriented repository of content and activities, which allows storage of XML content and all other formats, with descriptive and category metadata to facilitate retrieval.

(b) Integration of external content, portals, etc.

(c) Work- flow, lifecycle, process automation and security functions applied to the validation and publishing of content.

(d) Automatic indexing of unstructured content, automatic categorisation ot a taxonomy and automatic creation of taxonomies to provide content in context.

(e) Link management capabilities for maintaining relationships among elements.

Individuals and communities based management:

(a) Integration of tolls (charges of maintenance) for virtual meetings, virtual workspaces, virtual classrooms, discussions and group scheduling etc.

(b) Management of individuals, competencies, expertise, temporary and permanent groups/ communities.

(c) Peer- to peer information sharing.

Administrator based Challanges:-

(a) Monitoring and reporting for "Working manager," training coordinators, knowledge or content managers, etc.

(b) Management of resources and facilities for training and meetings etc.

All there genetic categorization is applicable to both corporate and public sector environments and it assumes that learning and information are keys to successful enterprises, regardless of their type.

Digital Rights Management

Digital Rights Management (DRM) has emerged over the past years as a matter needing careful consideration within the learning and information space agenda. Digital Rights Management is really about managing digital assets and as yet, there is no broad consensus on the scope of digital assets management required within the higher education environment.

It is encouraging that an alliance has been formed between the OLIS project team and the Knowledge Open Initiative (KOI) team based at Management Information Technology to embed the Documents Rights Management systems requirements within the broader Knowledge open initiative learning systems architectures, This will provide a "point-of engagement" for the stakeholders in universities, including librarians, to develop policies and procedures for effective management of digital assets. Most of the technical standards development work to date has concentrated on technologies for enforcements of rights, which is of particular concern to software vendors.

The global education communities however, represent a large creator and consumer network where enforcement represents only one aspect of the business. It is vital that there be international collaboration to develop an unambiguous statement on the nature of digital assets management for education communities and on the requirements for infrastructure of Document Rights Management System.

Portals

It is most important that librarians position themselves carefully in the protracted portal debate. Over the past couple of years the use of the term "portal" has broadened to cover a complex array of problems relation to resource discovery and access management. There are few special features of portals:

(a) "The fundamental distinction between searching for the known, as against the unknown, needs to be borne in mind constantly in the planning and evaluations stages,

(b) There is a basic difference between" window-shopping" and being able to "buy-what you-see."

(c) Most applications, by definition, will have a task-focussed portal to assist users;

(d) Most task-focussed portals have the ability to cover some, but not all, of the wider service spectrum portal space.

(e) The underlying portal technology ultimately depends on the use of directory services to match people and resources."

(f) The weaving of task-focussed portals into a single presentation layer for the user is a desirable goal.

(g) Cross-domain discovery still presents enormous challenges to the portal concept.

(h) The effectiveness of portals is inextricably linked to the application of metadata schemas.

(i) Users will continue to use multiple portals.

(j) The cost of maintaining portals is often underestimated."

In most cases libraries have assumed that the "information" portal is their province and often managed by other groups in the university contest, challenges this assumption, In general institutional mechanisms to deal with this area of activity remain weak and, in many cases, non existent. It is in this context that agreement on a high-level information model, such as that postulated by the Brandon-hall.com staff, becomes a pressing necessity.

Authority

The realisation of an integrated learning and information space is heavily dependent on underlying infrastructure for access management encompassing issues of authentication, authorisation and directory services. Progress in developing effective access management infrastructure has been slow for a number of reasons including:-

(a) Different "world-views" of the nature of the problem being solved between librarians and IT managers. At one part librarian access to global information resources and IT managers viewing it as being primarily a matter of security and access control.

(b) A lack of appreciation of the role of managerial services in terms of access management relation to consumers, resources and services.

(c) A preoccupation with institutional access management protocols at the expense of much needed distributed services architectures.

It is crucial that librarians continue to develop and articulate their access management requirements, but that they do so in the learning/information space, rather than solely the library information space.

The time is ripe for concerted action at the institutional level to integrate systems and services and to press for national and international collaboration on the standards and specifications necessary for global interaction between learning and information communities. The potential contribution of the library community is considerable but this will only be realized by adoption of a much broader view of the service spectrum and by engaging more actively with technical colleagues and with those responsible for delivering the learning experience.

2

Libraries and Growth of e-Learning

E-learning is becoming an influential force in higher education today: a force, which has some kind of presence on almost every campus and in an ever-increasing number of college and university courses. It is a growing and dynamic environment, one in which fluidity and change are the norm culturally, institutionally and technically. Within this environment, the academic library is still searching for a permanent, comfortable, and serviceable position that is enough to be flexible, accessible and continually up-to date with the wider structure of higher education i.e. university and higher learning institutions.

e-Learning has quickly evolved to include not only courses that are taught primarily online and over a distance, but also to include traditional "brick and mortar" courses that have been enhanced with electronic elements. In fact, these hybrid courses now out number distance-learning courses run by universities.

Course management systems have enjoyed an analogous growth and also moved swiftly from scattered implementation based on online classes to enterprise-wise services that support and extend the entire curricula and related institutional services. The traditional classroom activities with electronic elements is changing the way to access, create and use information by students and faculty. It is providing new opportunities for libraries to design and disseminate new services. On the other hand libraries create these new services and it need to highlight their expertise, abilities and irreplaceable resources in order to take a leading role in the new e-learning and course management environment.

The OCLC Programme

OCLC created e-Learning Task Force in the spring of 2003. The Task Force was comprised of representatives from the libraries, the administrations, the IT departments and the Instructional Design Support Groups at OCLC. Its members are American and U.K. colleges and universities. They joined hand and discussed e-Learning programme.

The members engaged in OCLC programmed reflected a diverse and complex range of approaches to e-Learning. And while there was no "one-size-fits-all" in terms of solutions to interactions between libraries and e-Learning environments, there were common themes in terms of the underlying institutional dynamics governing the current state of e-Learning.

OCLC programme gave its recommendations:

Learning Methodologies and Technology

The term e-learning no longer applies merely to distance learning, but also to more traditional courses that have incorporated electronic elements into the day-to-day teaching and learning process. The Task Force agreed that learning methodologies and technology have become linked and that the interrelationship among needs to be better understood and more radically reassessed.

Metadata and Repositories

In order for learning objects to have any kind of value, they first require the use of semantically consistent, easily found and transported between institutions and repositories. In fact, the management of digital asset repositories, learning objects repositories, and the metadata governing their use are inextricably linked, and the issue surrounding learning object repositories are equal to and a part of the issues surrounding digital asset repositories. Ownership, management and asset control are the three issues of prime importance. Such issues that in the digital world cross organizational boundaries and create institutional tensions.

Libraries are also interested in developing ways to integrate and expose (in a technical sense) their existing systems, resources and services in university-wide course management systems. One of the first possibilities for this integration is with virtual reference services.

Training

It stressed on the need of training for librarians, for faculty and for students. The challenge of establishing relevant, yet scalable training is not new to librarians and there is now the possibility of embedding training support within the learning managements system as a part of the learning activity. The idea of "just-enough-just-in-time-just-for-me" was seen as a desirable objective.

Collaboration

There is a need of collaboration work as a whole, not a part and work together amiably and constructively to create the complex standards and challenging technical solutions required for high-quality and cost-effective teaching. It requires collaborative mechanism and collective expertise of the library community to provide not only leadership, but also timely, cost-effective input to the development of institutional infrastructure and appropriately developed and placed services in proper way.

E-learning and Libraries

There are various terms that are used in providing instructional methods using Information Computer Technology, such as online education, E-learning, virtual classroom and some others. The online education refers to teaching and learning method mediated by a computer, but presupposes that there should be a connection to a computer system at place which is different from learner's personal involved in the design, delivery and managing instructions using computers. It not only involves the process of designing, delivery of instructions in different platform and managing instructions, but also the technologies of managing contents and training and authoring.

e-Learning in Distance Education

Distance education has emerged as a viable alternative to conventional class room education to achieve the goal, of education for all. It aims at providing enormous flexibility to learners and methodologies followed in providing distance education in various modes starting from correspondence to audio, video and telelearning. This way E-learning has ushered in or at least shows great promise as a suitable methodology for successful implementation of Distance Learning Programmes.

E-learning is becoming an influential force in higher education today; a force that has some kind of presence on almost every campus and in an ever-increasing number of college and university courses. It is a growing and dynamic environment, one in which fluidity and change are the norm culturally, institutionally and technically. Within this environment, the academic library is still searching for a permanent, comfortable and serviceable position that is possible enough to be flexible, accessible and continually up-to-date with the wider university structure.

Once synonymous with distance learning, E-learning has quickly evolved to include not only courses that are taught primarily online and over a distance, but also to include traditional "brick and mortar" courses that have been enhanced with electronic elements. In fact, these hybrid courses, as they are generally termed, now distance learning courses. In India there are 30% universities which are conducting hybrid courses. If one uses a more generous definition (a traditional course that keeps all its classroom session but adds an electronic presence), the percentage would be even higher.

Course Management System

Course management systems (software applications) have enjoyed an analogous growth. They have moved swiftly from scattered implementations that support a few online classes to enterprise-wide services that support and extend the entire curricula and related institutional services. During the survey it is found that in two years the number of courses using guess by 120% from 25 courses in 2005 to 29 courses in 2006. According to campus study of private universities hence have slightly improved between 21% to 30% in India. IGNOU established in 1985 to provide distance learning for the people for variety of reasons. A survey[1] explains that university is conducting the course of Library & Information Science programme, a Bachelor and Master's level. Since 1989 the methodology followed adopting printed study material, counseling reasons, software packages, online, CD-ROM search etc., seminars, Tele and radio conferences, audio-video and terms end examination. They used CDS/ISIS and WINISIS storage and retrieval system designed for computerized management of structured textual database assessments. Within courseware environments, faculty are able-at a minimum-to take advantage of a suite of productivity tools to distribute information to students and engage with students individually or collectively. At a moral sophisticated level, faculty can deploy a wide variety of communication, tracking and assessment tools. Course management programme also provide a collaborative workplace for students to work with each other. They are becoming a tangible place where the work of teaching and learning can occur. When strategically placed, courseware environments provide a logical place for information and knowledge to be created, assessed and used. Currently, vendors market courses management systems to academic information technology units or to individual faculty departments. Typically, libraries are left out of the decision-making and implementation processes. This way the libraries have the challenge of deploying their services in a new learning environment using a technology outside their control.

The enhancement of traditional classroom activities with electronic elements-epitomized by the rise of the course management system-is changing the way faculty and students access, create and use information. It is providing new opportunities for libraries to design and to disseminate new services. It is providing new opportunities for libraries to design and to disseminate new services. At the same time when libraries create these new services, they will also quickly need to highlight their expertise, abilities and irreplaceable resources in order to take a leading role in the new E-learning and course management environment.

E-learning offers libraries a powerful medium for reaching faculty and students directly as they engage in teaching, learning, research and outreach. In turn, this integration provides enriched services for an academic community that has used traditional library services and it offers a way to reach those faculty and students who have begun to ignore the library and go directly to the Web for their information needs.

The OCLC E-learning Task Force—OCLC created an E-learning programme in the spring of 2003. There were 15 member group engaged in this programme. OCLC included librarians, administration, technologists and faculty from the cooperative's academic institutions. Members represented institutions from across the continental United States and the United Kingdom and from the full range of institution types: research and doctoral universities, four-year standing arts colleges and community colleges. The group issued a white paper to aware with the outcome of OCLC programme and efforts made between libraries and E-learning environments.

The Institutional Context—It was a diverse and complex range of approach to E-learning with 'one-size-fits-all' for solution to interactions. There were, however, common themes in terms of the underlying institutional dynamics. It is obvious that the faculty, the libraries and the IT are equally responsible to design and develop the secure use infrastructure. But there are hardly few departments which have attained each strategic approach because there is no common shared language on which to build strategic initiatives. There have been many attempts with mixed success to overcome these barriers through organizational restructures aimed at convergence. Cultural barriers, including motivation to change, remain the major impediment in most institutions. Digital initiatives are an interesting example-all groups would have a distinct interest in almost any digital initiative. The main problem is service convergence, Identifiable common values and terminology are required to facilitate much more imaginative service solutions that transcend traditional organizational boundaries. The important task is to provide service from the student viewpoint is necessary based upon the notion of easy, convenient access to services at the point of use. It follows, therefore, that service convergence and interoperability of systems are interdependent concepts that must find manifestation across all parts of the institution independently of any particular organizational structure.

Effective Policy

There are views about lack of effective policy referred at various courses which develop the E-learning environment. The first is cultural economic model. Secondly the growing unease among senior level academic administrators over cost issues associated with E-learning and the difficulty in measuring its success. To date, most institutions have found that the deployment of E-learning increases rather than decreases costs and there are no recognized methodologies for assessing cost benefits. But the policy to "do it yourself" strategies predominate at the faculty level.

Learning Enhancement—Learning methodologies are now linked with technology, but little understood. It needs more research into the impact of on line learning techniques on the actual learning experience. Technology can be used successfully to enhance learning irrespective of the mode in which learning takes place. Moreover, online learning can be mixed with traditional learning methods and schedules, and thus the terms "blended" learning and "hybrid" learning now have widespread currency. The search, therefore, appears to be for balance and the aim is to provide an equitable learning experience for all participants, whatever the mode in which the learning takes place.

Cultural Barriers—There are cultural barriers to overcome in achieving such as aim. (1) The first reason is "invisible" nature of teaching processes in most academic institutions. Within the existing teaching culture the individual faculty member values autonomy and the ability to impart knowledge based on discipline-specific research interests. (2) Curriculum objectives are often not readily explicit and the notions of sharing intellectual property, (3) collaborative teaching based on technology and collaborative learning are not widely practiced. The advent of more sophisticated technologies and services, which are easier to access will provide greater flexibility and increase faculty confidence. These technological improvements help to stimulate more innovative ways of enhancing the learning experience.

Learning Objects—The term learning object was commonly applied to educational content by those involved at the systems development end of the spectrum, therefore required different metadata than that pertaining to the more static world of information objects.

(a) More recently it has become evident that learning objects have a life cycle that begins at creation and extends through preservation, with many intervening events.

(b) Learning objects will be shareable or at least will be reused or repurposed. This implies that they need sufficient identity to be discovered, located and accessed by education and learners. There has also been the assumption that learning objects need to be described in context indicating that the particular educational framework-inclusive of learning outcomes, activities and assessments-needs to be associated with the object in some immediately recognizable fashion. These assumptions indicate that instructional context is integral to any meaningful interpretation of a learning object.

(c) All these notions are combined into one data model in the form of the IEEE Learning Object Metadata Standard. It may cause implementation challenges have emerged. It led to these components (a) digital Assets (b) learning activities (c) secondary information. Digital assets can be described once and used many times much in the way that librarians describe information objects. It is too early to know how the learning activities will be developed as a conceptual and practical model but the application of technology to different components of generic learning activity should assist in developing such models over the next few years.

Metadata Strategies

Higher education institutions have been slow in learning about or adopting any strategies for the application of metadata to learning objects. While librarians generally have the most skills in metadata creation, they also have rarely been asked to apply those skills to developing and tagging learning objects and building learning object repositories. Faculty members, who are not as familiar with metadata and its uses as are librarians, do not in many instances see the need for metadata. This lack of knowledge furthermore can disapprove considerable reluctance and apprehension in releasing learning content for description to the library.

There are three primary cultural issues emerge pertaining to creating, using and tagging learning objects. These issues are:

(a) Ownership
(b) Management
(c) Access Control

Within an owner-centered culture, generally, the same group administers acquisition/creation, management and access control of the object. But learning objects and digital assets necessarily cross organizational boundaries and reside in a user/learner or patron culture as opposed to an owner culture. Operating under a user-centered model requires a different understanding and perspective on the three activities of acquisition.

Even in the most collaborative environments, the academic community has not addressed the differences between an owner-centered culture and a user-centered one not have these differences been redressed. Until the community recognizes and deals with this issue, there will continue to be serious challenges surrounding learning objects and metadata, semantic consistency and quality assurance.

However there is a desperate need for analysis of schema requirements, controlled vocabularies, taxonomies and the widespread adoption of application profiles that draw upon standard elements from multiple domains. The desire to share resources has generally been a driving force in developing application profiles in education worldwide. The relatively low priority that most academic institutions assign to the concept of shareability partially explains the slow adoption of metadata applications. There is, however, a growing realization within the academic community that digital assets and learning objects have value as an institutional resource as well as an acknowledgement that the sheer complexity of the emerging digital campus requires some level of managed control. Ultimately success will depend on the forging of working relationships between designers, producers, owners and consumers of metadata. In order to meet this objective, the academic community will require a much greater understanding of the way in which learning activities are created, used and supported in the digital environment and of the systems infrastructure that sustains these learning activities.

Integration of Library and Learning Management Systems Environments

Generally the library is keenly interested in integrating its systems and services into learning management systems environments. Unbundling existing systems configurations to allow more of a "plug-and-play" desktop environment is a key component to unifying services. Of equal importance is assessing service among the student engaged in a learning activity within the learning management system (or CMS) environment. This concept is not innate to the library environment that generally functions under a "pull" type service model, because students wish to search and discover from within the learning management systems environment and create dynamic information and learning sets of-the-fly. Integration efforts will have to accommodate these organizational and learning activities. Students and faculty alike require tools and services to access and partake successfully in information seeking and learning environments. Workshop participants unidentified systems requirements with both technical and functional aspects as well as requirements with both technical and cultural aspects.

Functional Requirement

(a) Display and integration of variety of information windows as part of a learning activity.

(b) Aggregate access to content in any given learning context.

(c) Bibliographic tools that permit easy searching and reference completions.

(d) Access to tools that render and present content in user-customized formats.

(e) Effective software into course management system to access reliability of contents.

Cultural Requirement

(a) Application of library resources in course management systems.

(b) Integration of third-party commercial information services.

(c) Customize portal facilities for storing personal preferences.

(d) Provide for easy access to virtual reference services at the point of need.

(e) Embed training modules to assist in information seeking.

Content Management

It is obvious that institutions are beginning to think in terms of digital content management or institutional repository management. But there is confusion over the term "repository", little knowledge of types of content management systems and the question how to manage institutional repositories.

Libraries need to reposition themselves to be viewed by the academic community that they serve as managers and observers of the repository space preservation and reusability of learning content are essential requirements in repository management, yet libraries were not much involved.

These content management systems are capable of incorporating multiple metadata schemas to handle various types of content. Librarians are well-suited to populate these metadata schemas with the appropriate terminology. Their expertise in aggregating content positions them to be active partners with the faculty in accessing content, in planning courses and in using course management applications. At the technical level, standards agencies are attempting to define the functional requirements of teaching and learning using managed content with a view towards developing appropriate technical architectures and standards for interoperability.

Technical Infrastructure

Each individual college or university with technical infrastructure is unique to that institution. Some institutions have a centralized information technology (IT) organization whereas others have a more decentralized one. There seems to be no necessarily consistent pattern. In the United States, libraries often support their own technical infrastructures, but the access to it (the network) resides under the control of a central IT group. Culturally, this situation can often cause friction and territorial tendencies may therefore surface. Infact IT departments and functions may or may not be centralized and the possible territorial frictions between IT and library systems architecture control, and the solutions for service convergence on a technical level will need to be highly customizable.

Training

There is a need of better and more focused training for both faculty and students. There is a need of involvement of libraries for improved and new information seeking skills. Online learning is to be a satisfying and successful experience. Librarians have to meet the challenge of establishing relevant information infrastructure. The idea of "just-enough-just-in-time-for-me" was seen as a desirable objective. But it needs collaboration among librarians, faculty and the instructors. Some way it is difficult as little known about the way students engage in learning through course management systems because there is little experience of embedding and thereby introducing auxiliary service into the learning activity. There are few training modules designed for collaborative development among institutions which may prove to be discipline-specific or even learning activity-specific.

Standards

There have been various important national and regional efforts making significant progress, but generally within the confines of their own particular regional or national groups. Thus, the search and development of specifications and standards for E-learning communities on an international level has a very short history beginning with the establishment of the IMS Global Learning Consortium (IMS). Considerable progress, however, has been made within IMS with a range of relevant specifications for key stakeholders within E-learning communities. The work was very systems-oriented, but later more focus was given on learning design. IEEE recently released the first and only real education standard, referred to earlier as the Learning Object Metadata Standard. As with all new standards, a great deal of attention is now being paid to making it a workable standard to be revised and extended in the light of feedback from practical implementations.

Strategies

Leadership and vision are needed to make E-learning a satisfying and cost-effective teaching strategy. In more practical terms there is a need for top-down and bottom-up strategies together with short-term and long-term strategic initiatives. Given the present policy vacuum in many institutions with regard to E-learning, the library community has major opportunity to articulate its requirements in the E-learning space. There is a need for a logical and well organised planning approach to managing existing and emerging digital assets. It is highly likely that there will be multiple repositories within any one institution, which will require metadata scheme and federated searching service to ensure specified levels of interoperability. It is also likely that the institutional repository infrastructure will need to interact with repositories in other institutions; therefore, there will be a requirement to offer services that support a distributed network of repositories across various functional and disciplinary domains. In other words, there is a need for conceptual and technical infrastructures that allow the library to offer pertinent service. At the same time the library should be well-positioned to update services as new opportunities and viable alternatives present themselves.

Collaborative Opportunities

There are two categories of opportunities (1) integrating existing and new library and institutional services into the E-learning infrastructure; and (2) managing digital asset repositories.

Both are not mutually exclusive categories; there are common services for both areas. We have already noted that the management of learning objects fits well under the general fabric of digital asset management.

Integrating Library Services

The requirements identified are below:-

(a) Consecutively display and integrate a variety of information windows as part of a learning activity.

(b) Aggregate access to content in any given learning context.

(c) Provide bibliographic tools that permit easy searching.

(d) Access to tools that render and present content in user-customized formats.

(e) Integrate adequate software into course management systems to encourage good practice and to assess reliability of content.

(f) Integrate third-party commercial information services.

(g) Customize portal facilities for storing personal preferences.

(h) Provide easy access to virtual reference services at the point of need.

(i) Strongly planned training modules to assist in information seeking.

It will be a key to success if links with library system vendors and learning system vendors, to articulate the functional requirements and to develop technical architectures and applications capable of supporting the library services as part of the learning activity. There is also a need to monitor the flexible (Changing easily) world of open-source solutions in order to sponsor and incorporate best practice developments within the generic infrastructure.

Digital Asset Repositories

Academic institutions will probably require infrastructure and services to support a range of systems all with their own particular capabilities for managing digital assets. These systems include:

library systems, course management systems, content management systems, learning content management systems, document management systems and archiving systems. Again, irrespective of the particular capability of the various systems, collaborative initiatives by the library community in developing common services infrastructure are key. Many of these initiatives relate directly to metadata support.

These common services include:

(a) Development of metadata schema and application profiles.

(b) Development and maintenance of vocabularies.

(c) Maintenance of registries for application profiles and vocabularies.

(d) Provision of centralized metadata and content repositories for learning objects.

(e) Value-added metadata service.

(f) Best-practice metadata development guides.

(g) Digital rights management languages and architectures.

(h) Metadata quality assurance services.

(i) Preservation and archiving services.

3

e-Learning and e-Learners

E-learning

The academic library community of Universities and other higher learning institutions has considerable expertise in off-campus delivery of information, both in exploiting its potential and problem solving. Involving the university library in course development and delivery will both lighten your load and add depth and richness to students learning.

Principles of E-learning

The principles on which an information service should be based are introduced in this section, and the following section describes how they may be developed into practice. These are the principles which institutions should apply to enrich the educational experience of eLearners and to ensure that courses are supported by appropriate information resources:

(a) Responsibility
(b) Quality
(c) Equity
(d) Access to information and help
(e) Information literacy
(f) Integration
(g) Communication
(h) Whole-process costing

Responsibility—Your institutions has a clear responsibility to ensure that E-learning is appropriately underpinned by good quality information. This applies both to core readings, and supplementary material to broaden and deepen understanding. Involving the library service in this is as vital with off-campus work as it is with on-campus provision. Over the past decade, universities and their libraries have recognized two key factors:

- Good information support contributes significantly to the quality of the educational experience of students.
- ' It pays dividends to involve librarians at an early stage and to treat information support as an integral part of course design.

Hence, from the outset, look to foster a close partnership with the library service in the planning and validation of the course. The institution should also make clear in marketing, publicity, and any other communication with prospective students, what they may expect in relation to library and information provision, including any financial implications for them.

Quality

The quality of library and information provision is as important to e-Learners as it is to traditional on-campus students. Monitoring and evaluating library provision should be integral to the quality assurance mechanism set up for the course itself.

Equity

The circumstances of e-Learners and/or the nature of the course may make it impossible to offer equal access to the wide range of services offered to campus-based students. However, e-Learners need information provision comparable in level and richness to that offered to campus-based students. This may require imaginative and unusual solutions. Librarians should plan this aspect together with e-Learners form the initial course design stage.

Information Literacy

All e-Learners must be given the opportunity to develop and enhance their skills in finding and using information. This not only ensures that they can fully exploit information resources for their E-learning course, but also provides them with a life skill, and with mechanisms for updating their knowledge after the course has ended. It is important to work with your librarians to embed information literacy training into the delivery of support for the course.

Integration

e-Learners should be aware how best to integrate library and information provision into the course in a flexible way, since the needs of different E-learning courses and of different students within a course will vary, depending partly on the nature of the individual course and partly on the prior knowledge and skills of the individual E-learner. It is needed to ensure optimum integration between the delivery of course materials and information support i.e.

(a) Technical plateforms for delivery of information

(b) The media mix used to package the information

(c) The balance between physical and electronic routes & media to information

Communication

Communication should underpin the relationship between e-Learner you and the library on the one hand, and between both and the e-Learner on the other. This applies at all stages:

(a) Designing and planning a course

(b) Marketing and student recruitment

(c) Delivery of the course

(d) Student progression

(e) Quality assurance

(f) Monitoring and evaluation

Whole-process Coating

Library provision adds value to any course and is an integral and enriching part of the student experience. It has to be costed like every other part of the course, with an emphasis on cost-effectiveness. When deciding whether a course is viable, realistic information support costs need to be taken into account and searching questions may have to be asked. If appropriate course cannot be delivered without unreasonable cost to the institution and/or the individual learner, the course may not be able to go ahead.

Plan

To assist providers in ensuring on appropriate library and information service for e-Learners, and in integrating such provision into course delivery, here is an initial checklist of questions:

(a) What information skills will e-Learners need?

(b) What information resources will they need?

(c) What level of help, advice and support will they need?

(d) How will these services be delivered?

(e) What are the financial implications for the e-Learners?

(f) What are the cost implications of all aspects of library and information provision?

(g) Who will be responsible for each aspect?

(h) Will e-Learners need to have access to a library close to them and how may this be arranged?

Considerable time and effort are needed to project plan, manage and co-ordinate the provision of library and information services, especially if this is the institution's first such venture.

An alternative model is to outsource some parts of the service to external partners or commercial service providers, such as educational technologies or suppliers of content. This adds a layer of complexity to the co-ordinate of the process, making careful planning, and allocation and ownership of responsibilities, even more crucial. Whichever delivery model is chosen, if it fulfill the overall responsibilities to the concerned students, the same issues arise.

Quality Assurance Framework

The library and information services are delivered within the quality assurance framework of the programme, the university:

(a) Access and monitor the information needs of E-learning students.

(b) Define service levels so that course providers, library and information services, and especially e-Learners, are all clear about the level of service to be provided and who will deliver it.

The library and information needs of e-Learners are similar to those of campus-based students, but the ways of providing services to meet those needs may be markedly (improvement) different. The library will help to benchmark service delivery for e-Learners against that for campus-based students as part of the planning process, thus ensuring that no key service is neglected.

Access to information—e-Learners need ready and timely access to a wide range of relevant information resources, whether for course-related study, wider reading or further research. Library will be providing them with content in the form of printed or electronic texts, or learning objects, for course work. You will also need to provide access to additional resources, in electronic form where possible. Here is a menu of media options:

Books—These may be useful as course texts and could be posted out to e-Learners. If they are to be paid for course fees, make sure that the costs are reasonable. A growing number of eBooks is available, and these may become and increasingly attractive solution, although finally agreed with licensing implications. A plenty of planning time may be allowed to investigate these options, especially if e-Books are not already embedded in your institution's provision.

Printed or Electronic Articles

These can be closely tailored to the course. They might consist of original content, or of journal articles or book chapters where copyright permission must be obtained or licenses negotiated, and a fee paid. Bear in mind the cost, and especially the artistic movement needed, for copyright requests. The costs may make some items uneconomic, and you will need time to find alternatives, Experience shows that you need to allow at least six months for seeking copyright permissions, whether the library or some other agency is carrying out this work. Often, your library can recommend alternative resources, which are already available, or other sources of copyright cleared materials, thus reducing the need to seek permissions or negotiate licenses.

CD ROMs or DVDs

These are valuable because they can hold a large amount of course reading, combined with other useful information and software packages, including self-paced training applications, without incurring online costs or the problems of insufficient bandwidth. Copyright and license fees may be payable.

Multimedia

The Learning environment can offer a wide range of multimedia enhancements to learning, such as embedded video-links, film clips, images, and sound. There are licensing, copyrights and cost issues, which again will take time to work through, Some multimedia can be presented on CDROM or DVD, if bandwidth is significant issue (of which more below). The co-manager here will be the university's media or IT services, or external suppliers, and increasingly libraries will become involved.

Electronic resources

A vast range of electronic resources is accessible via web, providing great opportunities for the e-Learner to read beyond course materials. However, the quality of web-based information varies enormously. Work closely with the library to direct e-Learners to appropriate resources, and to teach them to evaluate resources they discover for themselves. Important issues are:

***Network Access for e-Learners, Capacity and** Bandwidth.*

As a pre-requisite, e-Learners must have access to the Internet, but bandwidth is variable. See whether essential sources can be delivered via the web at acceptable bandwidth: CD-ROMs or DVDs may be preferable. Technical issues for which specialist advice is needed include the use of institutional firewalls, the need for proxy servers, and knowledge of how variable browser configurations and versions of software work and interaction practice. A small-scale pilots should be setup to test network issues, especially if multimedia material which is to be used.

Access to and Location of Resources

The links and access routes for the e-Learner depends on the location of the resources. For example, links to published resources. A combination of provision will probably be needed. As this is a very complex area, and no two institutions will necessarily arrive at the same solution. All sorts of practical considerations may guide you to right to take plan.

Authentication

Most electronic resources require users to be authenticated. National authentication scheme should be take up:

(a) e-Learners will be handled within the registration procedures of your institution.

(b) User names and passwords will be generated to provide access to library or computing facilities and services.

(c) e-Learners obtain authentication for the electronic resources you wish to provide.

(d) Information on user names and access requirements will be communicated to them clearly and accurately.

Document Delivery and Inter-library Loan Services

Most higher degree students will need to make use of document delivery services, which supply books, journal articles, conference papers etc. beyond the core readings of the course. There is usually a per item charge. Determine how much, if any, document deliver can be paid for out of course fees. Or how much the e-Learners themselves will be expected to cover, and how all of this can be regulated and managed. Commercial suppliers provide index or table of contents services, and documents can be ordered direct by e-Learners paying online by credit card. The university library may be willing to supply items from stick by post, but such a service is unlikely to be scalable or sustainable, and is therefore not recommended.

Access to a Local Library and Information Service

Negotiation access to a library to individual e-Learners will take time, and may require funding for fees or a reciprocal agreement. A university may be able to provide additional access to information or to help. Consider whether you can realistically negotiate access on behalf of the e-Learners, or whether you can provide them with guidance as to how they might apply for access to a local library themselves.

Access to Help and Advice

Help and advice for e-Learners in relation to their use of information should be integrated within the overall support planned for the course programmed. It is unlikely that you will be able to organise direct one-to one contact, 24×7 for these services. Instead, aim to provide the opportunities for e-Learners to become self-reliant and to take responsibility for their own learning. e-Learners will however, need individual help and assistance at different stages of their course. Decide how you can provide support, directly or indirectly, and consider the costs, practicalities, and scalability of such support. e-Learners will need information and advice on: IT, including networking connectivity, hardware and software support, using information resources, alternative library and information services.

Information Literacy

Information literacy has supermacy if transferable skills which are essential to the learner during the course, and also in their work and study afterwards. These skills include:

(a) Knowing where to look for information

(b) Creation efficient search strategies

(c) Evaluating and authenticating information

(d) Processing and managing information.

The collaborative efforts of librarian and educational technologists as appropriate in order to:

(a) Analyse what information skills e-Learners will need to develop during their course

(b) Embed appropriate training into the programme at various stages

(c) Produce on line information literacy courses, workbooks or module some of which should be interactive

(d) Include an information literacy module in the foundation or introductory course

(e) Create gateways or portals to guide e-Learners to selected and validated resources

(f) Integrate access to these services into the learning environment.

Information skills should be developed incrementally throughout the programmed. A key objective is to enable and assist eLearners to become independent, self-reliant and resourceful in their location, evaluation and management of information, i.e. to become information literate. Consider supplying CD-ROMs or DVDs or designing a website, to contain:

(a) A variety of resources and information for e-Learners

(b) Guides and handbooks to course material and the library

(c) Licensed software packages, such as word processing, spreadsheets and databases

(d) A web browser

(e) Packages of training tools.

Integration

Just as information literacy is an integral part of the learning outcomes of the course, information resources must be integrated into course delivery. For example, Integration of resources in learning environment, the library website, gateway or portal, and publishers' and other external databases, is a very complex area and IT services. e-Learners need to transform quickly and efficiently to information resources, which are located on a variety of servers around the world. Only careful planning will enable this to happen. Some issues to consider are:

(a) Whether individual items of e-Content, are embed such as articles, images, sound bites and film clips, in the course materials, or will you make links to them from the course materials.

(b) Where will these resources reside: on the central controlled server, or on and institutional or library sever, with access via gateways or portals?

(c) How other resources, will be linked such as e-Journals, e-Books, or bibliographical or image databases, some of which will be located on publishers or aggregators, servers? Your library may already have access to software, which makes use of open reference linking, which will simplify this process.

Management and integration of resources and links is essential, to ensure that a complex and hybrid network of information resources is made as simple, Logical and transparent to e-Learners as possible. There is no single solution, so allow plenty of time to plan what works best in your circumstances.

Communication

Good communication support the relationship between e-Learners and course and service providers. It is vital for managing and clarifying the expectations of e-Learners, and for ensuring the effective planning and quality management of the programmed. As a minimum:

(a) Involve the library at the outset, and on a continuing bases, to identify information resources and delivery mechanisms

(b) Include references to library and information provision in communication with e-Learners

(c) Clarify service levels with the library. For all aspects of access to information, help and advice, and communicate these clearly to e-Learners.

(d) e-Learners are more likely to be satisfied with the services provided, and this must be made clear to them what is and what is not, available.

Process costing

Well-designed and well-managed library and information services will add value to the educational programme and to the e-Learners. They must be affordable and cost-effective. Try to identify the whole, direct and indirect, capital and recurrent costs, for every step. This includes:

(a) The purchase or licensing of resources, and copyright fees, as required

(b) Associated staff costs of obtaining or negotiation these resources

(c) Designing and delivering online information literacy training

(d) Designing, managing and maintaining gateways and portals

(e) Providing help and advice to e-Learners

(f) Specific costs related to any e-Learners who wish to visit the university library in person, of fees payable to enable them to use a local library.

If these costs are affordable, scalable and sustainable, and think the balance of costs providing a mix of printed and electronic resources for core or for further reading, the comparative costs will help you make decisions among:

(a) Printed or electronic books, including costs of purchase, posting or licensing

(b) Printed or electronic study packs, including costs of photocopying, copyright clearance, or licensing

(c) Document delivery, at a cost per item, including copyright clearance; consider the need to manage or ration supply.

The balance between quality of provision and affordability may be a delicate one, but e-Learners have the right to expect high quality library and information services and resources, failing them in this respect will undermine the course. The actual funding model adopted to support e-Learners is ultimately less important than informing them fully about any financial implication in undertaking a course, and ensuring the support.

Library and information services will best contribute to the richness of the e-Learning experience when:

(a) The institution offering the course takes responsibility for enduring that the library and information needs of its e-Learners are met

(b) Quality and assurance mechanisms assess the supporting material, including the library and information provision, as an integral part of the course provision

(c) Access to a wide range of high-quality information and support, including flexibility of access in technical and temporal terms, is offered to the e-Learner

(d) Information literacy is developed as an integral part of the course, to transform e-Learning into a rich, challenging and individual experience for the independent learner

(e) There is effective communication between the library and the course designer, and between the provider of information services and the e-Learner

(f) Costs are properly identified in respect of library and information service provision along with all other aspects of the course

(g) Provision is optimized by building on the institution's existing information resources and services.

U.K. Libraries

If we overview the U.K. libraries, in particular UK university libraries have a long history of successfully providing library and information support to distance learning students. The techniques, experience and creativity exploited in meeting the needs of distance learners can now enrich the design of library and information support within E-learning.

Until the 1990s, the two main providers of distance learning programmes in the UK were the Open University and the External

Programme of the University of London. Students were provided with the materials they needed to complete their course of study in published or course pack form. Some university extramural (extansion service) departments also provided loans using 'book boxes' delivered to remote classrooms for part-time students.

From the early 1990s, and onward many more UK universities began offering distance programmes, particularly at postgraduate level. The adoption of quality assessment mechanisms within the sector consolidated concern for the support of distance learners. The procedures of the Quality Assurance Agency ensured that the needs of distance learners could not be given less weight than other types of learner. An increasing number of libraries developed dedicated services for distance students, such as:

(a) Telephone renewals
(b) Literature searches
(c) Photocopied articles
(d) Postal book loans
(e) Individually negotiated reciprocal access arrange-ments.

However, new technologies were emerging and changing, and the Internet soon emerged as an opportunity to begin fashioning the digital library. The UK Joint Information Systems Committee (JISC) was quick to begin sponsoring research. It established a large number of projects focused on the delivery of remote services under the E-library programme, which ran from 1955 to 2001. The first two phases of e-Library involved 100 UK higher education institutions and disseminated knowledge of many of the issues and techniques relating to e-Library support widely across the sector: e-Library resulted in a number of sustainable services which can be used by designers of support for e-Learning. For example, HERON, www.heron.ingenta. com, offers a national service for copyright clearance and digitization of book chapters (Book contents) and journal articles. Equally, the resulting knowledge base and widespread good practice within UK university libraries is an important resource available to course designers.

However, libraries began exploiting the new technologies to reinforce their existing provision: developing websites, email support, conferencing, access to e-Journals and databases, and online information skills tutorials. Such services were key components of the Open Library, (www.open.ac.uk/ library) developed by the Open University, and the dedicated Distance Learner Support Units established in university libraries. Wider students access to physical library space in the UK has been facilitated by UK Libraries Plus, a reciprocal scheme which allows distance learners and part-time students from one member institution to use the library facilities of another.

This experimentation has resulted to successful provision of library and information support to e-Learners is completely integrated within the e-Learning curriculum and environment. It cannot easily be added once the course has been designed.

The UK university library sector is generally very well placed to support the integration of library and information provision within E-learning, and to continue the dialogue with course designers as E-pedagogy develops. This is partly the legacy of its long and successful experience of supporting distance learners, and partly a consequence of its enthusiastic and cooperative adoption of new solution provided by rapid technological development.

4

e-Learning—A Synchronous and Synchronous Tools

Fundamental paradigm shift from teacher-centric to learner-centric learning. From a scenario where the teacher is a decision-maker, with the instructor merely action as the facilitator. The traditional system of learning assumes the teacher as one predict and facilitator. It requires training for every individual and learning is certainly not a one-time activity and the traditional approach is quite inadequate.

Approaches

There are many approaches available depending on a specific requirements. (a) Web-based training could be either synchronous or asynchronous, (b) the learner studies at his own time and pace, (c) he can log into the system at any convenient time. Synchronous on the other hand means that the learner and the instructor synchronize their timings so that the learning is guided and structured in a certain format by the instructor. This enables real-time interaction not only between the learner and instructor but also with a peers and experts. The best form of synchronous learning is obviously in an instructor-led classroom. If learning is on the web and it needs to be synchronous, then there are multiple tools and technologies available – audio and video conferencing, text chats, shared whiteboards and so on. Synchronous training through the web is capable of overcoming a number of problems where critical training inputs can be imparted just-in time from experts at remote locations. The cost benefit analysis of such an exercise needs to be done on a case to –case basis. What we need to understand is that it is possible to judiciously combine asynchronous and synchronous tools and provide a relevant, cost-effective solution.

At the heart of the system lies the LMS (Learning Management System). This will need to interface with authoring tools for content creation. The process of content creation per se is a very involved one, requiring subject matter experts, instructional designers and tools, visualizes, graphic designers and so on. Content needs to be delivered and tracked and performance monitored and evaluated. Depending on whether learning is completely online (which assumes good connectivity), part of the content might have to be made available offline, either through a download or through CDs. The learner data might have to be interfaced with a other back office systems within an organization. The different categories of people interaction through the Learning Management System would be the content providers, administrators, tutors, experts and of course the learners.

Depending on the vendor, the technologies used could be different and they would follow their own architectures for implementation. But generally there are three layers. To begin with, there is usually a 'learning object repository' that houses all the content. By content one obviously refers to multimedia content which could be text, graphics, images, audios, videos, etc. There is the middleware component in the form of 'learning object brokers' This operates between the tools layer and the learning repository- a software layer that maps data in and out of the learning object repository. Finally the data is displayed in the browser window and this could use various technologies like DHTML, ActiveX controls and so on.

Content Creation

Content creation by itself is a vast area. There is a widely held misconception that authoring tools take care of everything that has anything to do with content creation. This presupposes that many activities would have taken place prior to this. This include user profile analysis for setting training goals, curriculum design for translation training goals into learning objectives, instructional design, story boarding, and courseware design for carrying the learning objectives forward into session plans, modules and courses. Today there are tolls that automate most of these tasks. Use of templates for content creation greatly enhances both ease and speed of large volume content generation.

Administration

Any training system whether manual or online has an inevitable administrative element associated with it. In the case of Web-based systems, this includes facilities for on-line registration, enrollment, maintenance of different user profiles and associated access rights. It also takes care of the security issues and some event provide facilities for billing through an e-commerce component. Other important aspects would be facilities for replication across multiple servers and locations, installation, configuration and customization, and other housekeeping jobs like archiving. This module would include course administration well and therefore provide the necessary user interface to the application administrator for going about all these tasks. It would also provide interfaces for other user profiles like tutors and experts to track student progress and generate necessary reports.

The Benefits and Limitations of E-Learning

The field of employee development and training is undergoing a sea of change due to the many new forms of technology that are becoming available. Web-based learning, CD-ROM training and interactive computer simulations seem to be the wave of the future. Currently, it is possible to learn many different kinds of skills on the Internet. Websites like trainingnet.com offer a wide range of business classes on-line. CD-ROM training now offers movie-quality lectures by famous business authors and consultants that include a variety of quizzes and exercised. And computerized simulations allow jet pilots and surgeons to practice their skills in the safety of the computer lab.

These types of e-Learning can be useful in number of ways:

(a) Employees at various sites can also learn the same thing at the same time;

(b) People learn what they need to learn and go at their own pace;

(c) Computers are very useful at repeatedly testing people until they learn a particular thing.

Computer are particularly useful for cognitive learning, i.e. the kind of learning that deals with logic, concepts and memorizing technical words or foreign languages.

It seems that computers are generally best for individualized learning. But even so, sitting in front of a computer screen simply can't take the place of a group learning situation for many topics. For example, you can't really duplicate the experience of live brainstorming on a computer screen. There are a growing number of programs and Websites that allow people to do that, but it's just not the same thing. The people's faces and voices, as the brainstorming becomes more exciting. Yet that excitement creates a kind of synergy and momentum in the group's energy that is really essential.

These kinds of skills simply cannot be gotten from a computer screen or a CD-ROM. They come from practicing with other people, e.g. trying a certain behavior, making mistakes, getting feedback from others and then trying again.

5

e-Library : Learning Environment and Teaching Development

Information Technology Update

The old GE50 mainframe computer soon became a dinosaur as computers went through wave upon wave of innovation. Any of today's desktops or laptops is far more powerful and faster than that early GE50. Coded instructions on paper tape gave way to batch processing via 80-column cards, which in turn gave way to typing instructions at an individual workstation, to today's pointing and clicking in a windows-like environment. Developments in the near future are likely to see finger interaction replaced by voice communication.

There are recent trends in IT:

(a) The days of videotape are numbered.

(b) DVD has replaced CD-ROM as a storage medium.

(c) Dial-up access to Internet service providers has been overtaken by broadband connections.

(d) The world of photography has changed markedly as still print and slide cameras have given way to digital cameras.

(e) Laptops are giving way to a new generation of powerful pocket PCs, Palm Pilots, and PDAs.

(f) The world has become googlised as we use google for information.

(g) The occupation of door-to-door encyclopedia salesman has passed into history as their DVD counterparts or virtual copies on the Internet have replaced hardbound encyclopedias.

(h) Bankbooks and chequebooks have become casualties of Internet banking.

(i) The personal letter has almost disappeared having been replaced by instant SMS messaging on mobile phone.

Changing Paradigm for Schools

Information and communication technologies have the potential to change. We are witnessing a paradigm change in our schools-from teacher-centred to learner-focused. As ICT becomes integrated into every aspect of a school's activity. UNESCO's 'A planning Guide' succinctly captures the changes in student and teacher roles in the newer kinds of emerging learning environment. These changing roles of teachers and students have been aptly summed up in the quip that teachers change from being "sages on the stage" to becoming "guides on the side".

Changes in student and teacher roles in teacher-centred and learner-centerd learning environments resulting from ICT integration

Learning Environments	
Teacher-centred	***Learner-centred***
Student role	*Student role*
(a) Passive recipient of information	(a) Active participant in the learning process
(b) Reproduces knowledge	(b) Produces and shares knowledge, participates at times as expert
(c) Learns as a solitary activity	(c) Learns collaboratively with others
Teacher role	*Teacher role*
(a) Knowledge transmitter, primary source of information, content expert, and source of all answers	(a) Learning facilitator, collaborator, coach, mentor, knowledge navigator, and co-learner

Teacher-centred	*Learner-centred*
(b) Controls and directs all aspects of learning	(b) Gives students more options and responsibilities for their own learning

Along with changed student and teacher roles, ICT is contributing to changing the whole structure of schools. 'Closed door' classrooms are stretching their walls to embrace the wider community; the instructional emphasis is moving from memorizing facts to inquiry-based learning; rigid class timetables are becoming more flexible; and technologies once firmly located in schools are being accessed from beyond the perameters of the school. More than any other previous technology, ICT are providing learners access to vast stores of knowledge beyond the school, as well as with multimedia tools to add to this store of knowledge.

The UNESCO handbook's incredibly wide coverage – embracing educational technology of the mind, the new literacy, multiple intelligences, wearable computers, goals of education, information objects, the mathematics of informatics, and much, much more – details the potential of ICT to impact on every aspect of the life of schools, changing them irreversibly from schools as we now know them. The real potential of ICT is the way it changes learners, which brings us to e-learning.

Today nearly anyone is familiar with e-mail and progressively we are becoming acquainted with e-banking. We also hear about e-commerce, e-business and e-trading, and so it was almost inevitable that the term e-learning would be coined. e-learning in one Internet search engine and receive 13,929 hits (AltaVista). In another search engine, receive a staggering three and a half million hits (Google) – even more hits in both search engines if the variant e-learning spelling is added!

As a market activity in commerce and industry, e-learning has been enthusiastically accepted by the corporate sector. "Corporate e-learning is one of the fastest growing and, most promising markets in the education industry"

The delivery of content via all electronic media, including the Internet, intranets, extranets, satellite broadcast, audio/video tape, interactive TV, and CD-ROM.

e-learning is a broader concept [other online learning], encompassing a wide set of application and processes which use all available electronic media to deliver vocational education and training more flexibly.

It is useful also to separate e-learning from distance learning, which generally includes text-based materials as well as electronic media. These relationships between e-learning, online learning, and distance learning are seen graphically:

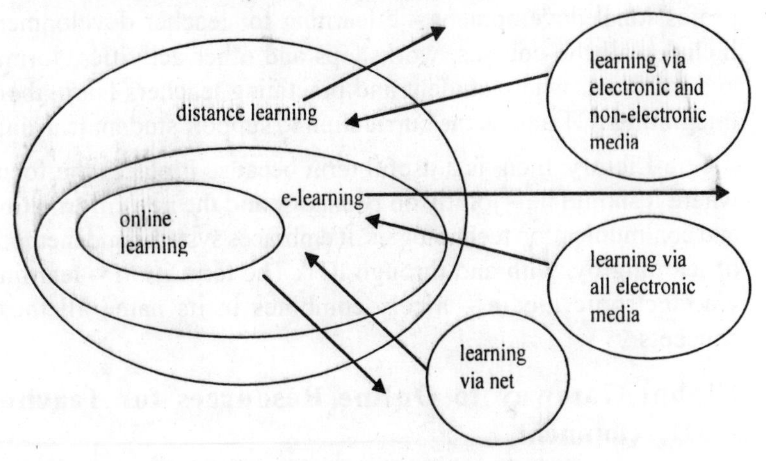

The relationship between online learning, e-learning, and distance learning

The above figure shows that e-learning is broader than online learning since it includes all electronic media, like CD-ROM and DVD for instance, both of which are off-line media, as well as web technologies. At the same time, e-learning is a sub-set of distance learning, which also utilises print media.

Information and Communication Technology

UNESCO described the term ICT as the tools and the processes to access, retrieve, store, organise, manipulate, produce present and exchange information by electronic and other automated means. These include hardware, software and telecommunications in the forms of personal computers, scanners, digital cameras, phones, faxes, modems, CD and DVD players and recorders, digitised video, radio and TV programmes, database programmes and multimedia programmes.

In so for as ICT include hardware, software and telecommunications, ICT is seen to be the means to support student learning via electronic media. E-learning, then, is the growth in students understanding and knowledge when they utilize ICT in instructional settings. Thus in the context of teacher development – both the initial training of teachers and their continuing professional development – e-learning for teacher development includes all the courses, workshops and other activities, formal and informal, where student and practicing teachers learn about integrating ICT across the curriculum to support student learning.

e-Library, then, is a useful term because it places the focus where it should be – jointly on pedagogy and the new information and communication technologies. It embraces systems and methods of learning by, with and through ICT. The term itself – learning via electronic media – nicely combines in its name all these concepts.

Global Gateway to Online Resources for Teacher Development

The world's most popular Internet search engine, Google, announced (19th February 2004) that it had added a billion pages to its gigantic store of 4.28 billion pages. A problem arising from this growth is how to sift through the enormous number of 'hits' that result from most search queries Not only is the number of hits far too many to look far too many to look at in a single lifetime but many of the web pages in Google's vast database are of dubious quality, or may even have changed location or disappeared since being indexed.

A practical solution to the problem of too much information is the emergence of global gateways to online knowledge networks in particular fields. These global gateways might be more familiarly known as web portals, although a large number of other terms are in vogue – information portals, super portals, vortals, hubs, networks, directories, digital libraries, virtual libraries, and clearinghouses. These terms all refer to a single access point or website to which users can go for particular information, and sometimes, as well, for a range of other services such as news, weather information, and discussion forums.

Whatever the term used, global gateways provide a necessary filter to help reduce information overload. Even more importantly, the filtered information has been evaluated before placement, and often links to sources and resources are accompanied by brief descriptions or annotations. Like the rapid growth in information, the number of web portals has similarly increased markedly in recent years.

Six web gateways from around the world are overviewed briefly below. Between them, these portals provide links to a rich source of e-learning materials for teacher development.

Selected education web gateways from around the world

Web Gateway	*Developer*	*Particular Focus*
(a) ICTs in Education (b) Education Network of Australia (c) Institute for Information Technologies in Education (d) Multimedia Educational Resource for Learning and Online Teaching (e) Knowledge Resources (f) National Grid for Learning	(a) Distance education and ICT (b) K-12 schools, vocational education and training, higher education (c) ICT in education (d) Higher education (e) ICT for education and teacher training (f) K-12 schools and teacher education	(a) UNESCO, Paris (b) Educational, Adelaide (c) UNESCO, Moscow (d) California Street University, Los Angeles (e) UNESCO, Bangkok (f) British Educational and Communications Technology Agency, London

Online books, theses, research publications and newspapers (a) Education and ICT research publications (b) Education research theses (c) Electronic books (d) Online newspapers	Online education journals (a) Education across the curriculum (b) ICT in education and teacher education (c) Libraries and archives (d) Research in education
Policy documents, reports and databases (a) ICT in education (b) ICT in teacher education (c) Open and distance learning	Resources for teacher educators (a) Online tools (b) Web teaching/learning materials Other education portals (a) Distance education and learning (b) Teaching, teacher education and ICT

Multimedia Educational Resource for Learning and Online Teaching and e-Library.

The resource material collection in libraries is designed primarily for students and faculty in higher education institutions. Access is free though registration is required if adding to the collection. To be included in the collection, materials are peer reviewed and rated, placed into categories, and briefly annotated. Links are then made to the materials themselves, which can be located anywhere on the Internet. A useful additional description is called Assignments, which are designed to indicate how the particular materials might be used in a course.

I-SITE (Information SITE)

This site will help you to find in the internet the materials concerning information technologies in education. Every information system of this kind is similar to the specialized bibliography which connect you with the source as quickly as possible. This site permits you to find the more adequate "bibliography" and to continue searching there...

As Assignment is a detailed explanation of how an instructor has used a learning material. In addition to the text of the assignment, the assignment from contains Learning objectives, Pre-requisite skills and knowledge, Educational level, Technical requirements, and other information necessary to contextualize the use of the material. These examples are provided to help faculty understand a variety of ways the material might be integrated into a learning environment.

The categories of materials include Education and Science and Technology, along with Arts, Humanities, Social Sciences, Business, and mathematics. A typical entry in the Education collection is the following:

Information Literacy competency Standards for Higher Education

Author: Association of College and Research Libraries (ACRL)

Information literacy standards for higher education were developed by the Association of College.....

Location: http://www.ala.org/acrl/ilcomstan.html

Registered users can add materials (to be reviewed), comment on materials in the collection, and add Assignments. When users register, they are invited to indicate their broad interests. They may then see which other members have similar interests and, it they wish, communicate with them by e-mail.

Knowledge Resources

This comprehensive UNESCO gateway contains several components that are highly pertinent to teacher education and e-learning, in particular its collection of web portals and its virtual library.

Web Portals

The growing list of portals includes those developed by the UNESCO (Bangkok) Regional Bureau, as well as those developed by other organizations. The most relevant portal in ICT is for Teacher Training.

(a) *ICT for Teacher Training*: This gateway to Internet resources and websites, dedicated to training teachers in utilizing information and communication technologies to enhance their teaching skills contains sections on: (a) ICT in Education, (b) Teachers Roles in the ICT Ervironment, (c) ICT Training Strategies and Online Courses, (d) Integrating ICT into Teaching, (e) Teaching Ideas, Lessons and Curriculum Materials, (f) Educational Software/ Courseware, (g) Using Internet Resources, (h) Electronic Collaboration, (i) Bringing Your Classroom Online, and (j) Evaluation Tools and Indicators.

Virtual Library

The Virtual Library contains links to a wealth of worldwide electronic information resources, from many different sources, on topics dealing with education, social and human sciences, culture, and communication. This website facilitates virtual access to library resources without being physically present in any library or information resource centre.

The Virtual Library contains links to a wealth of worldwide electronic information resources, from many different sources, on topics dealing with education, social and human sciences, culture and communication. This website facilitates virtual access to library resources without being physically present in any library or information resource centre.

The Virtual Library offers over 1,000 website links to bibliographic, full-text and statistical databases in specific subjects related to various aspects of education, social and economic issues, gender, population, social, science, culture, health, HIV/AIDS, and related areas. It also contains links to libraries and archives; full text electronic journals and periodicals; Internet references; and reference materials such as atlases, encyclopedias, dictionaries and maps.

National Grid for Learning

The National Grid for Learning is gateway to a large network of selected websites that offer high quality content and information in a wide range of areas: learning resources, games and quizzes, lesson plans and worksheets, reference material, libraries and archives, museums and galleries, and learning opportunities.

The resources are organized into user groups across K-12 and further/higher education, and also by broad subject category. The range of learning resources is extensive, for instance, an online course on using the Internet, courses and tutorials on use of software such as Photoshop and Illustrator, and collections of resources to support teaching of al subjects in primary and secondary schools. Similarly, users may access a wide selection of lesson plans and worksheets, including games and tests for all school subjects and many at the tertiary level too.

e-Learning and Teacher Development

Knowing about global gateways or portals to online resources can help key decision-makers with responsibility for teacher development who may be asked why e-learning is important. Additionally, it is useful to consider the changing emphasis in the national goals of education in countries around the world, In all UNESCO Member States, there is a realization of the role education plays in making the transition to an information economy in order to contribute and prosper in the globalised context of which all countries are now part.

Whatever stage of development in the use of learning technologies that teachers around the world have reached, there are new ways of storing and manipulating data and information that will influence individual intellectual development.

Teachers and lecturers use data and information as basic building blocks to assist learners to develop conceptual knowledge. As a result, engaging with technology can enable teachers and learners to store, view, manipulate and present information in many new ways.

Therefore, e-learning for teacher development must play a key role if rational education goals for education are to be achieved, thereby changing schools as we have known them in the past from predominantly teaching institutions to learning institutions. Many educators describe these changes as nothing less than a transformation of education.

6

e-Library for the Knowledge Society

It focused on the following interrelated action areas: people, infrastructure, online content, applications and services, policy and organizational framework, and regulatory framework. It included-

(a) quality teacher programs for professional development activities to renew teachers' skills;

(b) the computer technologies for schools project which provides surplus computers and IT equipment for schools; and

(c) the customer focused portals framework which saw the establishment of the education portal being built.

Work in Information and communication technologies (ICT) skills and education continued through the implementation of Learning for the knowledge society on the following priorities.

(a) facilitation and promoting collaboration in the education and training sector to improve ICT awareness and skills;

(b) ensuring that teachers and students have the necessary ICT skills;

(c) monitoring the equity implication of ICT developments, including the effective use of ICT by disadvantaged groups;

(d) pursuing the connectivity and telecommunications needs of the education sector including affordable high speed internet access;

(e) ensuring a coherent national approach to interoperability and common standards.

e-Learning and Students

e-Learning, like e-commerce, e-living and other similar terms are manifestations of the knowledge age facilitated by ICT tools and accompanied culture. In other words e-learning as the use of new multimedia technologies and the internet to improve the quality of learning by facilitating access to resources and services as well as remote exchanges and collaboration. However, a key element of e-learning and other terms is to collaborative environment in which they thrive. An example of an e-Learning activity can be one where a group of city students could be collaboration on a science project with students in rural areas or overseas.

Like the tolls and machinery of the industrial age which improved productivity and quality of life, e-learning is important because it has the potential to revolutionize teaching and learning– transform learning into a lifelong activity producing a skilled and ready workforce capable of adaptation to rapid economic changes driven by innovation. It is possible to describe the 'old' education system, the one we are moving away from, as one which prepared students for work in as industrial society.

Society and its multiplicity of components is one static-it is dynamic and ever evolving. Innovation has driven technology and technology in turn demands innovation. In any era we find education has been closely aligned to the prevailing socio-economic system. In the midst of the 'knowledge age' society demands and expects our education systems to produce creative, innovative and flexible students able to quickly adapt to taped socio-economic changes. The e-learning model is closely aligned to the needs of the current socio-economic climate and is providing students with the fundamental skills commanded by the 'knowledge age'. The knowledge age values and rewards ideas- for the first time in history the greatest source of wealth is in ideas.

(a) Raising the standards and improving attainment- by applying self-paced individualized and interactive material to improve individual support to learners.

(b) Increasing retention and improving outcomes-by utilizing personalized online guidance to allow learners to take greater responsibility for their learning.

(c) Broadening choice-by offering new subjects and new learning methods to meet individual needs.

(d) Increasing access to learning for disadvantaged communities- by making use of ICT tools and connecting learners to others, thereby reducing isolation.

(e) Removing obstacles to achieve-by providing new creative ways to motivate and engage learners of all abilities.

Fundamentals

Fundamental to e-Learning is empowering the learner and educator. The shift to the new paradigm is accompanied with educational benefits, which includes.

(a) Individual learning for all learners, including the disadvantaged, disabled, gifted and those needing special curriculum.

(b) Collaborative learning is facilitated through access to a range of online environments – enabling learning fro other individuals or groups of learners, leading to the development of cognitive and social skills of communicating and collaborating.

(c) Tools for innovation-e-learning is accompanied by a suite of tools to enable teachers and learners to be innovative, creating and sharing ideas or customizing digital learning resources for their own use.

(d) Flexible study-learning anytime, anywhere- blending traditional and innovative methods to meet learners' needs.

(e) Access to online communities of practice- the Internet can bring learners, teachers, specialist communities, experts, practitioners, and interest groups together to share ideas and good practice, contributing to new knowledge and learning.

There is a need to 'reconceived the role of teachers and teaching'. There was a need to redefine the role of teachers and teaching in the process of e-Learning. The role of the teacher as the 'knowledge authority' or as the transmitter of information is in danger when access to a wealth of resources is available to individual learners. Access to abundance of information diminishes the role of the teacher as the 'all-knowing ' figure. In the 'e-world' the role of the teacher becomes one of a learning guide who is there to facilitate. Supporting this view, Spender informs us that 'teachers are no less important in the new system... but teachers will play an entirely different role when the students can do their own leaning, at their own pace, at their own place'.

There are following teacher roles in e-learning environment:

(a) Teacher as learner in the classroom-teachers are accepting that students might do better in special fields and are more ready to learn with and from them.

(b) Teacher as tutor-the tutor's role is not just the subject expert who facilitates learning, the tutor facilitates communication, and is a coach, consultant, referee, assessor and helpline, the tutor as a guide and monitor, bringing parties together as manager, provider or broker.

(c) Teacher as collaborator with students- in ICT based activities the teachers tend to participate as peers together with the students.

(d) Teacher as developer- teacher develops learning materials mainly in electronic format.

(e) Teacher as researcher-teachers researcher of own educational experiences as a way to reflect and internalize the innovations promoted in the classroom.

(f) Teacher as lifelong trainee-ICT literacy is the first step in the professional development of teachers.

(g) Teacher as member of a team of teachers- in distributed e-learning environments teachers are 'members of a team of teachers'

However the position of the teacher has shifted from the 'one in charge' to a partner in the development of students. In many aspects the teacher and student roles become interdependent. As one takes on a specific role, the other takes on a complementary role. Nevertheless to be effective practitioners in this new environment, teachers will need to be adaptive, flexible, and willing to be lifelong learners themselves.

A key competency is simply 'problem definition' which defines what kind of information is needed, from where it is accessed and how to process the information as well as its presentation and management. Other competencies needed to enhance ones knowledge and critical thinking skills include:

(a) technology literacy- the ability to use new media to access information effectively;

(b) information literacy- the ability to gather organize and evaluate information and form valid opinions based on the result;

(c) media creativity- the ability to produce and disseminate content to a range of audiences;

(d) global literacy-the ability to interact and collaborate successfully across cultures; and

(e) literacy and responsibility- competence to consider the social consequences of media from the standpoint of safety, privacy and other issues.

EdNA Online

It was developed in 1994. It is a database providing online services. Initially called the EdNA Directory Service and later (1997) renamed EdNA Online in recognition of its wider function of facilitation networking opportunities and provision of interactive services beyond resource discovery and information retrieval. Today, the service has mature to be an institution in e-learning, innovation and application of cutting edge technologies. Organised around Australian curriculum and competencies, EdNA Online is a gateway to freely available curriculum support recourses and communication tools. EdNA Online is the only site in the world with the following features:

Features

(a) Targeted at users in all sectors to education and training;

(b) Publicly owned and provides its online resources free of charge;

(c) Provides a national knowledge node in an increasingly complex system of knowledge networks with in a federated system;

(d) Provides both information about education and training (a directory function) and resources to support curriculum;

(e) Provides specific resources and tools to support and utilize the Internet in teaching and learning, while also providing resources for all subject/ discipline/industry areas;

(f) Promotes collaboration and networking through its communication tools;

(g) Offers access to specialist collections and online activities through its 'related sites';

Functions

Resource discovery—It is an educational gateway to quality online educational resources and services, EdNA Online has a database of;

- Over 17000 evaluated, value-added online resources.
- Access to quality assured international collections including;

EdNA Online also provides flexibility for the teacher at school. Utilizing new technologies a teacher can select and link to specific EdNA categories of resources or create and save a search on any subject. Such packaging of resources by the end user, in this case the teacher, combined with other activities, facilitates the organization of research where learners can work on their own or in groups and the teacher adopts the role of the facilitator, rather that the authority.

Interactive services—A key feature of e-learning is interactivity. EdNA Online over the years has incorporated a number of interactive services to foster collaboration and information sharing among the education and training community. Its suite of interactive services includes;

(a) Regular general and sector specific newsletters,

(b) Its noticeboards disseminate information about conferences and events and share knowledge and resources to communities of interest. Current notice boards include library books for schools, museums and galleries news and events, resources on appropriate and safe use of the Internet and others.

(c) It also provides interactive tools which foster both synchronous and asynchronous discussion, while the chat room provides a virtual real-tike environment for sharing information.

(d) It is a communication tools also enable the dynamic development of e-learning communities. These communities promote virtual collaboration that is focused on addressing specific topics. Communities of practice use these tools for various reasons.

Therefore EdNA Online provides our national e-learning environment with descriptive quality content that can be packaged and repackaged to provide multiple access points to information. Its browse pathways enable access to topical resources which can be utilized by subject specialists and combined with other learning activities provide rich learning experiences for the learner. The interactive tools foster and encourage online communities to thrive and provide support for their participants, along with enabling national and international collaboration.

e-learning offers a new range of skills which are essential for every discipline at every level and for life and work, enabling people to contribute and benefit fully as citizens. As learners make use of digital environments they acquire and practice a wide range of e-oriented skills, such as information literacy, online collaboration-all important life skills.

(a) Establish and extend online knowledge networks;

(b) Reconceived the role of teachers and teaching;

(c) Leverage resources to enhance online knowledge networks'

(d) Demystify online education an training services;

(e) Maintain pressure on issues of technology access;

(f) Develop ICT skills for education and training personnel across geographical and organizational boundaries;

(g) Establish seamless global learning framework; and,

(h) Create greater public awareness of the benefits of online knowledge networks.

7

e-Learning—A Financial Study

There are two major problems that had complicated distance learning's progress for almost a decade had been solved.

1. Students and administrators believe that the quality of e-learning now matches that of traditional teaching methods.
   (a) Three-fourths of academic leaders t public colleges and universities believe that online learning quality equals or that online learning quality equals or surpasses face-to-face instruction.
   (b) The larger the school, the more positive the belief in the quality of online learning compared to face-to-face instruction.
1. Universities provide distance learning to users, with a rate of increase of about 25 percent per year.

Greater acceptance and use of e-learning today and fewer reservations about its quality. It seems too good to be true. Innovative approaches like UMassOnline,by aiming for larger audiences and returning profits directly to academic institutions, will gradually allow nonprofit e-learning to pay its way more successfully. It is suggested that it will encounter consistently decreasing returns on e-learning investment as an inevitable result to the strategic model employed in most post secondary education. Three distinct challenges demand solutions if traditional universities are to successfully confront the economic realities of distance learning:

(a) First many traditional universities are not willing to draw useful lessons from the more advantageous financial and IT models of for-profit or other nontraditional institutions.

(b) About a third of e-learning is accredited by professional bodies, and many programs have relatively high per-class student limit; some have no limits on per-class enrollment.

(c) The production of course content by full-time university professors is not guaranteed. Growing evidence indicates that many career-minded faculty are skeptical of investing much time or effort in developing online learning courses, believing the effort to be low in yield both financially and intellectually.

E-learning at traditional universities does not stint on the quality of the education process, but nontraditional and for-profits cut corners. Any one carefully reviewing the current results for many of the leading nontraditional institutions will find that quality and service meet or exceed that of their traditional peers, however with significantly smaller class sizes, more sophisticate online resources, and excellent acceptance of online degrees by prospective employers.

The role of an adjunct at a traditional university is ambiguous and often controversial. It's a university-like to have disproportionately high course loads in distance learning or classroom instruction where the professor is a part-time hire, not a member to the full-time faculty yet the financial advantage is clear.

Higher education has known for decades that substitution cheaper labor for more expensive labor reduces instructional costs. The use of graduate teaching assistants, adjunct and part-time faculty, and other instructional personnel has enabled institutions to keep their costs from rising beyond what they are now. The knock has always been that our dependency on part time faculty reduces the quality of instruction, and anecdotal evidence seems to support that view. The academy, broadly, worries about institutions that rely too heavily on adjunct faculty for two reasons: (1) the academic program may fall into the hands and control of administrative who make decisions based on financial expediency rather than academic quality; and (2) quality assurance may be difficult to maintain, since the academy has neither the infrastructure nor the culture to support a close monitoring of all places at all times and disenfranchised adjunct faculty.

The traditional university might also put extra emphasis on locally popular online programs, of course, while limiting the use of technology in others.

Saving on Overhead

From my perspective, one of the least appreciated aspects of the non-traditional model is that very large enrollment revenues make it possible to offer extensive services and support in online courses. Enrolments of hundreds of thousands of online students involve different return-on-investment (ROI) rules from those of a few thousand or less-numbers typical even of large traditional universities. The latter can't spread IT and courseware overhead as successfully as large online institutions and so face an inherent disadvantage: lower service levels for students and higher unit costs.

The advantage of sharing overhead also applies to factors such as availability of library resources, consistency of educational materials, class size, availability of online technical help, and so forth.

Hence, High-revenue nontraditional institutions offer a financial and service model that is inherently difficult for a traditional university to adopt without a fundamental change in strategic outlook. Putting aside some of the less important issues having to do with the logistics of course delivery, the greatest difference can be described in two words adjunct faculty. All of the large, successful nontraditional programs depend on instructors who expect no office space, benefits, plans and other perquisites.

Faculty Concerns About Course Development

The professor has a unique role in a traditional university. She or he is the centre of intellectual activity at the institution and thus the nexus of course development. Universities have a three-pronged approach to evaluating professors: research, teaching, and service, with research frequently accorded the greatest emphasis in tenure evaluations. The crucial question in the context of e-learning is whether full-time faculty are willing to prepare suitable material for use in online instruction.

The reluctance of some full-time faculty to participate in e-learning can be traced to several causes :

(1) there is a perceived loss of research time because of the work involved in developing and teaching online classes,

(2) many faculty members feel that the financial reward structure for e-learning is not commensurate with the amount of work involved. There are few, if any, financial inducements for participation in e-learning programs. Faculty should rank the positive and negative attributes of e-learning on a Likert scale, and noted the reward system as among the top-ranked deterrents. A third area of unease among full-time faculty is the quality of courses.

Another troublesome issue involves the intellectual property (IP) rights for online courses. An argument can be made that each instructor "owns" the slides, TV lectures, CD-ROMs, special course techniques, and so forth. The legal issues associated with faculty Intellectual Property concerns add additional overhead to the total per-course cost.

Nontraditional schools are minimally concerned with the Intellectual Property issue because many of their courses offer considerable teaching material to the professors beforehand to reduce the preparation time required. This, combined with outstanding technical resources, makes the development of learning materials less a controversy and more an opportunity to get a busy pert-time teacher the tools needed to prepare a course much more easily. When the university supplies most of the course material, Intellectual Property is not a controversial issue.

Traditional universities will find it difficult to deliver a full-scale distance learning program at a competitive price without making changes in the financial model employed.

There are more accredited e-learning graduate programs. About a third of the students are enrolled in professionally accredited graduate programs, up from a year ago. Nearly all online programs in nursing and library science are accredited. Business courses are by far the most popular and have the most accredited institutions – but the lowest percentage of students in accredited graduate programs.

Graduate E-Learning Enrollments in Universities

Program	*Regional Accreditation*	*Regional and Professional Accreditation*	*Total Students*	*University of Delhi*
Business Management	24,374	2,270	26,644	11,675
Education	17,715	8,290	26,005	7,507
Engineering	2,705	3,699	6,404	2,305
Library Science	433	2,643	3,076	790
Nursing	74	5,887	5,961	1,315
Public Health	3,351	950	4,301	997
Total	48,652	23,739	72,391	24,589

Possible Solutions

At the popularity of online learning increases, a two-level system seems to be emerging. Many traditional universities use e-learning extensively but are reluctant to set up full-scale online programs. This is particularly true of the top-level academic institutions which do not appear on any of the high-volume e-learning lists. This group faces an unavoidable fixed cost that is difficult to amortize without extensive use of adjunct faculty or a commitment to higher student volumes. The other level, a group of for-profit and not-for-profit nontraditional institutions, offers full-scale online programs in popular disciplines like management, engineering, education, nursing, and library science.

Virtual University

A far more drastic idea that could yield extraordinary benefits to student learners even in the short term is to establish a global virtual university. The concept is closely related to the four-university coalition just suggested, but it would involve many more institutions and students.

Currently, it's difficult for a student in one university to take an online course from another institution and get full credit. There are rules about budgeting, entrance requirements, allocation of student revenues, and other issues. The strategic vision here is a no-nonsense virtual university, where the procedures really have teeth – much tougher than the plans frequently proposed in state legislatures and other bodies. Many previous plans offer options but no specific directives. They fail because the various segments of the virtual academy are not willing to share revenues, academic prerogatives, syllabus development, established structures, and other traditional academic expectations.

Brick-and-Mortar Versus Blended Learning

Because of the relatively difficult task of duplicating for-profit universities' cost model and the equally difficult challenge of attracting more full-time professors to become involved in e-learning, it seems that another answer might be for universities to think outside of the box in a big way. One possibility is a different approach to capital budgeting: a direct trade-off of bricks-and-mortar investments for virtual learning development. The effects of this could be much higher classroom occupancy rates and fewer new buildings needed.

Much of the burden here would fall on the shoulders of faculty, since a large number would need to be recruited to participate. University administration would have to deal with the real challenge of trading capital construction amount in some cases for investments in leveraging e-learning. A large university could potentially save millions of amount a year in costs of building new structures and costs associated with maintenance of those structures, and considerably more in reduced unit costs per course, even after paying faculty for participation.

The major obstacle at traditional universities to offering distance learning is financial. Traditional delivery methods are inherently cheaper than technology-enhanced ones, and always will be under current university staffing norms. Perhaps the habit of using relatively few adjuncts for e-learning courses could be reversed and a new cooperative efforts of part-timers established.

Costly

However, there is an easier solution, far less painful that any of the approaches already suggested: Accept the status quo as a valid approach to online learning programs at traditional universities.

e-Learning is a financial loser in the long term except at extremely high revenue levels. This assumption ignores an obvious fact of life at any institution of higher education-e-learning is a necessary, a significant convenience, an indispensable service, and a way of life. So it's possible to continue what most universities do now: take their totality at the budget table but resolve to offer e-learning where it fits the institution strategically. This is not necessarily a strategy of capitulation – some of the drastic measures described to achieve profits from e-learning programs might not justify the difficulties they could cause on a traditional campus. In such cases, accepting the necessity – and the un-recovered costs – of developing and offering online learning programs makes sense.

8

e-Learning and e-Library

Electronical (digitization) refers to the conversion of non-electronic material to electronic form. A wide variety of materials such as conferences and workshops reports, research articles and theses and dissertations and other materials as diverse as maps, manuscripts, moving images and sound may be digitized. Digitization offers great advantages for access, allowing users to find and retrieve materials.

This therefore makes e-libraries the "right arm" of e-learning. If the classrooms are going out of the traditional face to face system, then the library has to take on the same face. e-learning needs a e-library to back it up. e-libraries will help the library reach all its users, both on and off campus, because one book soft copy/digitized can be accessed by more than one reader, which is not the case with hard copies.

e-Learning

The interactive use of ICT to facilitate learning is what is popularly referred to as e-learning. This is in line with the University's vision of delivering quality teaching, research during the ever increasing demand for higher education. It is worth noting that efforts to implement e-learning are a result of a broader global information age revaluation by the integration of ICT in the way we live. Goals of e-learning at universities are to improve the quality of graduates, by utilizing modern instructional materials and methods including use of ICT in teaching and research. It provides greater access to university education by developing capacity for increased enrollment through non-conventional approaches in teaching and learning i.e. distance education and virtual university. Among the many attributes of e-learning are that it is dynamic, collaborative, flexible.

ICT Policy : universities are having an ICT policy in place, designed to make sure that all users (students and staff) utilize the available ICTs efficiently and for the sustainable benefit of all. It is the universities e-learning policy "to experienced faculty/unit effectiveness and enable easier access to and coverage of university education by using ICT in instruction, learning and research through the university wide implementation of e-learning. This policy also provides for the development and maintenance of appropriate skills for the workforce. This is especially vital in IT because of its dynamic nature. There is continuous change not only in the skills needed but also the Technologies. In the same change the policy provides for the automation of the library.

e-learning provides opportunities to solve issues of time and space limitations; reach out to many users and ease the achievement of the millennium; access to information made efficient and effective. More information can be generated, accessed or retrieved within a shorter period; readers will be able to access local and international information sources to supplement their information needs; browsing possible; document delivery; acquisition of material without necessarily buying.

Virtual Learning

Open and distance learning has evolved over the years from traditional mode of print based delivery to virtual mode of borderless education system. Such education system are characterized by high level of ICT dependencies, collaborative arrangements and subject spread from conventional to innovative need based vocational and professional offerings. The institution support is towards guidance and certification. There are other modes like partnership or joint ventures, consortia and multi-agent provider. ICT is looked upon as a central requirement for any educational institution, that in open and distance learning systems.

Following are the important issues need to be considered for virtual learning environment for open and distance learning:

1. Problem of digital divide – In the e-learning context access to internet is most crucial requiring serious attention to provision of optimum bandwidth reaching out to the learners located at remotest corners of the world.
2. Technology requirement – From the design of a website to creation of a robust virtual learning environment multi-pronged analysis of technological requirements is a must. ICT supported environment for teaching and learning normally implies significant institutional change.
3. Standardization and Quality assurance – Most e-learning standards can be categorized into metadata, content packaging and learner profiles. E-learning standards are being developed by four main organizations – AICT, IEEE, IMS and BIS. In virtual delivery of learning resources, standards are important as they facilitate interoperability of systems, content and metadata.
4. Challenges of Open Source and Open Access–Open source applications based on free exchange of ideas and collaborative creation model is revolutionizing open and distance learning scenario and paving a way for innovative models for teaching and learning. Many open and distance learning institutions are now adopting open source applications as a major part of their development strategy. On the knolwedgeware front, Learning Metadata Standards and CMS applications like Moodle, ATutor etc. are becoming very popular and many open and distance learning systems are adopting them. In many cases popular applications like BlackBoard or WebCT are being replaced by open source applications. On the courseware front, many national and international institutions all over the world are now working towards the development of Open Educational Resources (OER) which is revolutionizing the content creation and delivery process.

There are eight different ways of learning based on forms of intelligence-linguistic, logical-mathematical, musical, spatial, bodily-kinesthetic, naturalist, interpersonal and intra-personal. Curriculum developers therefore, need to have a clear cut understanding of the learner requirements. Individuals usually rely on those modes to process information at an unconscious level, but may be consciously aware of the modes they prefer. We process visually (by sight), auditorally (by sound), kinesthetically (by moving), and tactilly (by touch).

Studies show that single-style classes can be more effective than classes with diverse-style learners.

Gagne's nine steps are necessary for planning for a virtual learning environment.

S. No.	*Instructional Event*	*Internal Mental Process*
1.	Gain Attention	Encourage activates receptors
2.	Inform learners of objectives	Creates level learning expectations
3.	Encourage recall of prior learning	Activate short term memory
4.	Present the course content	Selective perception of content
5.	Provide learning guidance	Semantic encoding for long term memory storage
6.	Imformation Performance through practice	Responds to questions to enhance encoding and verification
7.	Provide feedback	Reinforcement and assessment of correct performance
8.	Performance assessment	Retrieval & reinforcement of content as final evaluation
9.	Enhance Retention and Transfer to the job	Retrieval & generalization of learned skill to day to day applications.

Virtual learning is a combination of learning service and technology that provide high value integrated learning; anytime, anyplace. Standard components of virtual learning environment generally have one of the following components or a combination of these:

(a) ***Learning Management System*** (***LMS***): It is comprising tools that are used to plan, implement, and assess a learning process.

(b) ***Content Management System*** (***CMS***): It includes content authoring, sequencing, and aggregation tools that allow content to be structured in an instructionally sound manner to facilitate the learning process.

(c) ***Learning Content Management Systems*** (***LCMS***): It is an integrated system with features of the above two learning environments.

(d) ***Learning Content Metadata/Repositories***—Standard features of present day virtual learning management systems include:

  (a) Student registration
  (b) Content delivery in multimedia formats
  (c) Course scheduling and organization
  (d) Management of class transactions
  (e) Assessment and evaluation
  (f) Student tracking and report generation
  (g) Content assembly and authoring tools
  (h) Virtual and collaborative learning tools

e-Learning Tools

Marshall etc. have categorized e-learning tools three types:

(a) ***Curriculum tools*** comprising instructional tools, administrative tools (file management, authentication and authorization) and student tools (browsing of course content, collaboration and sharing through synchronous and asynchronous modes of communication, progress mapping and tracking).

(b) ***Digital library tools*** that support learners to access right information amidst huge amount of digital information resources available at the right time.

(c) ***The knowledge representation or concept mapping tools***: Concept maps and other forms of spatial semantic displays are evolving as alternative to traditional linear representation of information and as the basis of effective learning strategies.

Indian Scene

IGNOU's Initiative

IGNOU has recently embarked on two major initiatives towards developing virtual learning environment for distance learners – eGyanKosh: a national digital repository and Sakshat a one stop education portal of the Ministry of Human Resource Development (MHRD).

eGyanKosh

e-GyanKosh is an effort towards developing a national digital repository of learning resources. In the first phase IGNOU course materials are being digitized for uploading on the repository. This will be followed by incorporation of course contents of other Open and Distance Learning (ODL) institutions in the country. e-GyanKosh has been initiated with the following objectives in mind:

(a) to develop a digital learning content repository in a standard format

(b) to provide just-in-time access to learning resources 24′7

(c) to create metadata for searching and browsing of learning content through multi access points

(d) to help in long term maintenance and preservation of learning materials

(e) to facilitate sharing of resources among educational institutions and thereby eliminate duplication of efforts

At present a centralized model of implementation is being carried out where servers are located at a central location in the IGNOU campus and content is being digitized and uploaded in the eGyanKosh division of the University. There are making efforts to the decentralized structure so that other ODL institutions may contribute upload material on the repository online. The content and the metadata will be moderated at IGNOU centre before uploading on the repository. Moreover, a long term plan is being formulated to distribution. In the distributed model the repository will have an interoperable architecture with the facility of cross collection federated searching. The repository has the following features:

(a) Multiple media
(b) Searching and browsing facility
(c) Seamless search facility across collections
(d) Access rights management with usage tracking facility
(e) Multilingual database – Unicode compliant

At present the repository comprises Self Instructional Material (SIM) in PDF formats and Audio/Video programmes available on streaming server.

Sakshat: One Stop Education Portal of MHRD has been developed at eGyanKosh division of IGNOU. The portal was inaugurated on October 30, 2006. The portal envisages providing one stop solution to educational requirements of learners ranging from K to 20 covering all fields of study including vocational education and learning for life skills. The Objective of the Portal are:

(a) to provide barrier-free web based learning resources;
(b) to develop a repository of world class interactive multimedia learning content;
(c) to provide online platform for interaction through synchronous and asynchronous modes;
(d) to hone skills and knowledge through online mentoring and testing services;

(e) to monitor progress of scholars and other learners based on the performance in customized online tests;

(f) to facilitate learners in making informed decision on choice of profession through online career counseling facility;

(g) nature those who aspire for excellence.

Sakshat portal has been developed in two versions – one by IGNOU and other by NIC. The website developed at IGNOU. It has three tier architecture with the following three integrated modules:

(a) User interface

(b) Content management system / Learning Object Repository

(c) Administrative module

The user interface has the following five functional modules:

(a) Educational Resources: to help the learner available on the web in the form of e-books, e-journals, digital repository, digital library etc. Most of the sources collated are open source material;

(b) Scholarship: about scholarship opportunities through newsfeeds and announcements;

(c) Testing: enable the learners to test and upgrade their skills and knowledge through online testing;

(d) Superachiever: this is a special facility for those who aspire for excellence;

(e) Interact: Provides a platform for the learners to interact with their teachers, mentors and peer group in real time and for interaction includes, e-mail, weblogging, webcasting, online chat, discussion forum.

The user interface also has an inbuilt virtual class facility, rich with multimedia learning resources.

The content management and the learning object module is a collaborative platform developed for teachers to uploading content on the Portal. It is reviewed online by the Content Advisory Group identified for the purpose.

The Administrative Module function for user registration; setting parameters for online testing; user tracking; content management; maintenance of discussion forum, announce-ments, chat rooms; content uploading.

e-Learning as a Media

Learning can be thought of as how we direct ourselves, while education is that which is directed at us. Usually in education we concentrate on five steps :

(i) First generation deals with oral tradition of experience, best practices

(ii) Second general gave rise to formal education processes that eventually gave rise to today's educational bureaucracy.

(iii) The third generation of learning process started as the dominant formal educational paradigm.

(iv) The fourth generation of learning started after the invention of printing press.

(v) The fifth generation of e-learning took place to provide a positive paradigm shift for students in traditional educational program and a new source of education to those who are geographically disadvantaged.

The term e-learning or e-education has brought a new meaning to education. Its culmination brings the substitution of the conventional memory based learning system. The fast development of e-learning has become inevitable, and has given the wide spread acceptance to the internet as a vehicle for knowledge transmission, channel of communication, and information retrieval. E-learning means getting education via the electronic media. But learning, internet, can now reach masses of learner at their own convenience of time and space with minimal cost.

Therefore, e-learning has a significant impact on today's educational community.

E-learning enables learners gaining knowledge through the individual use of electronic or digital media such as computers, tapes, CDs, the Internet etc. There are two dimensions of e-learning, namely, on-line learning the learners achieve learning through the media of the Internet on Intranet, a term also equivalent to WBL (web-based learning), secondly offline learning is a means by way of an independent computer can be contents of the learning material stored on discs or CDs. Much better skills are required to maximize the potential of electronic resources as compared to those required for searching printed sources. Society is transforming into a new structure where the binary digit has become the foundation and basis for thinking. Chen (2002) also viewed that academic units and enterprises have veered from traditional in-class learning to limitless e-learning to meet the demand for more learner – centered environment.

e-learning is supposed to include a series of courses, involving computer-based learning and web based learning. e-learning refers to extensive application of computer based training, web-based training and virtual classroom using the Internet. e-learning connects the web through the media, using all kinds of electronic or digital appliances, including all types of computers, domestic appliances, mobile phones, PDA etc to allow learners to acquire up-to-date knowledge at anytime anywhere. e-learning perform the following functions:

(a) Exploration the tools provided by the Internet for learners to explore information.

(b) Experience the learning experience provided by the Internet for learners in all areas that encourage learners to explore self-learning.

(c) Engagement the innovative ways of learning provided by the Internet for learners that help the learners engage in cooperation, and cultivate awareness of community.

(d) Ease of use the availability of easy, digitized learning environment and the handy tools provided by the Internet to learners.

(e) Empowerment the content, manner, the degree of the progress of learning provided by the Internet to learners.

Impact of e-Learning

e-learning through e-mail has widened the scope of learning students' who clear their doubts their doubts about assignments and other course related materials. In this regard internet is becoming breakthrough technology to enter to the new millennium. Access to computers-connected communities has an impact on education with increase in software programmability, increased interaction, communication, shared visualization, and experiential learning, educated workforce, shared vision and collaborative creativity.

e-Learning Framework

There are seven dimensions of e-learning framework namely:

(a) institutional

(b) management

(c) technological

(d) pedagogical

(e) interface design

(f) resource support, and

(g) evaluations

(a) ***Institutional dimension*** – It is divided in three categories: administrative affairs, academic affairs and student affairs. (i) Administrative affairs deal with needs assessment, readiness assessment, organization and change, budgeting, partnership, programme, course information catalogue, marketing, recruitment, administration, financial aid, information technology services, instructional design and media services, (ii) Academic affairs deal with accreditation policy, instructional quality, faculty and staff support, work load and compensation and intellectual property rights. (c) Students affairs deals with pre-enrolment services, orientation, faculty and staff

directories, advising, counseling, library support, tutorial services, students newsletter, internship and alumni affairs.

(b) ***Management dimension*** – Management dimension deals maintenance and updating, information and knowledge management, scheduling, students performance records and security measures.

(c) ***Technological dimension*** – It examines issues of the technological infrastructure in e-learning environment. This includes infrastructure planning, hardware and software. It deals with the infrastructure planning, standards, metadata, hardware and software application.

(d) ***The pedagogical dimension*** – It refers to teaching and learning. This dimension addresses issues concerning content analysis, audience analysis, and goal analysis, medium analysis, design approach organization and learning strategies.

(e) ***Interface design*** – This design encompasses page and site design, content design, navigation, accessibility and usability testing.

(f) ***Resource supported*** – This dimension emphasizes instructional/counseling support, technical support, career counseling services, other online support services.

(g) ***Evaluations dimension*** includes both assessment of learners and evaluation of the instruction and learning environment.

The digitized society makes time faster and space closer.

Features

(a) Digital format is based on digital technology. Multimedia is used as one of the e-media to create some artificial matters with all kinds of virtues/values.

(b) E-learning provides a cyberspace for mutual communications from every where at any time.

(c) The information technology acts as a stimulus to the business growth in all fields of politics and economics, enterprises, medical educations, welfare, environment, research activities and others.

(d) Internet access in e-learning globally.

(e) It obtains high capacity content in a short time via high-speed line/cable.

(f) Interactive communication/interfaces smoothly.

Methods and Materials

While making survey on e-learning projects a short questionnaire may be prepared with the following points

(i) Age group

(ii) Gender

(iii) Experience in computer handling besides class course

(iv) Percentage of marks obtained in last examination

(v) E-learning is easy for access than traditional form of teaching

(vi) E-learning having more utility in day to day activities

(vii) E-learning is more reliable and cheaper than traditional teaching method

(viii) E-learning invites more participation in the educational programme

(ix) E-learning saves time over traditional method

(x) E-learning is used to be more helpful to the teachers than students.

It is used to analyse the students' requirement with a five point scale and administered students.

Components in designing e-learning—Our educational system networks, is built on three dimensions. (i) Objective (ii) subject content and (iii) learning modes. The learning mode has six components:

(a) Distance learning

(b) Search engine

(c) Using simulation technologies

(d) Using videoconferencing system in collaborative environment like instructional presentation question-answer, multi-multi-sites telecommunications.

(e) Cooperative efforts

(f) Coordinatior among different organization or fields

Limitations of e-learning as a process of teaching method**—** Self-learning has some disadvantages because learning is left entirely to the initiative of the individual. The success of learning depends on the motivational level of the learner, where social impact of poor groups in learning and personal development affects adversely. E-learning can help in reducing the time required on campus for practical experiments. The effectiveness of course on presentation skills, might be limited without practice in front of instructor or classmates. Therefore e-learning courses must be designed to facilitate student interaction as a matter of course.

Initiative efforts for e-learning

The new knowledge created by the communication revolution and supported by Internet have accelerated speed in work and action and demands constant quality improvement and innovation almost in every sphere of human activity. The knowledge and expertise of an individual becomes obsolete as speedily as machines and thus require to be upgraded with new knowledge. The expertise of an individual is neither static nor lasting in knowledge based societies. A large number of people in developing countries are illitrate and hence not able to derive benefit of knowledge boon. Knowledge is like light, weightless and intangible. On the hand knowledge societies demand life long learning and on the other hand many people in developing countries are not able to get adequate opportunities for education. A massive challenge before developing countries is to change the mindset and encouraging and motivating the people to learn.

The growing global e-learning programmes may promise quality education for every citizen of the world.

e-learning involves the use of some form of electronic media to provide access to educational content and enhance the learning process. Sometimes confused with distance learning, courses are believed via 'e-learning' when technology is used to bridge both an instructional and a geographical gap, often in concert with face-to-face communication. e-learning is: 'a range of activities, from effective use of digital resources and learning technologies in the classroom, to a personal learning experience enabled through individual access at home or elsewhere. Combined with established learning experiences, it can provide individuals with new and exciting opportunities to realize their academic and creative potential at their own pace'. Thus, e-learning is essentially the facilitation of teaching and learning via the use of some electronic medium.

As a result, interactions can be more useful and to-the-point, discussion can stay more on-track, and people can get a chance to craft their responses, group collaboration, new educational approaches, integration of computers, no age limit and flexibility. While e-learning will not entirely replace traditional face-to-face delivery of training content by education institutions. It enhances the learning process, and increases reach.

learning offers cost effective learning opportunities to several learners. In most instances, as long as e-learning can provide equivalent or better outcomes (retention of knowledge, demonstrably better skills, or higher levels of problem solving) at the same or lower cost than traditional training, then the convenience of e-learning and its ability to reach a wider audience will often win out. Teaching and learning appropriate–suits the styles of the learner; Interactive and user friendly; organizationally appropriate; new enough to generate interest and enthusiasm; and capable of being speedily altered and rapidly delivered.

Features of e-learning

Features of e-learning that have begun to emerge are as follows:

(a) We must continue to focus on the outcome of learning.

(b) Different learning outcomes require different skills and ways of acquiring those skills.

(c) Humans require interaction in order to learn well. Interaction is a human enterprise that technology may only partially be able to support.

(d) Training, the imparting of skills and commercial judgment

(e) Learning styles by culture e-learning will also tend to dominate the style.

The Internet is the medium which provides access to e-learning. The increased access to the Internet and greater bandwidth are both expected to increase as a number of individuals moving into online learning. Broadband availability increases the speed of Internet access and does away with the frustrating low quality of waiting for web pages to download which is a disincentive for the learning process.

Training and competence building are regarded as the pillars of a successful sustainable development procedure. There are millions of people who require training to upgrade their skills and the existing experts cannot meet training requirements of such a large number of people through face-to-face training.

The world has evolved substantially over the last two decades. The common usage introduction of computers, accompanied by the onslaught of the Internet revolution has changed the rules of the game. Contrary to common perception, mere access to computers and electronic networks is not enough to ensure that developing countries will be able to participate actively in the knowledge economy.

It is our argument that teachers constitute the right group to establish new technologies, and e-learning in particular. If education and capacity building are critical steps for entering into the new global economy, e-learning should also be considered a critical facet of basic development, an alternative medium of capacity building, and a means to people's empowerment. e-learning is especially attractive because people can log on in their homes, while in the developing world, the learners still need to go out of their homes, and still pay too much for Internet access.

Technologies to enable e-learning have tremendous potential for India. However, the benefit of these technologies must be made available to the rural masses of India, otherwise, they will only widen the digital divide. Various technologies have been used over the years to spread distance learning including he radio, TV, and now the Internet. There are several problems which affect rural India but amongst them, a major problem is that literacy amongst farmers and rural folk of India is very low. Emerging technologies such as Natural Language Interfaces and the Next Generation Internet will enable several innovative applications in e-learning and enable parallel learning by helping to break the cycle of literacy followed by computer literacy.

Successful Implementation of e-Learning

e-learning needs new and emerging, simple, and scalable technologies, it can provide an alternative teaching and learning solution, with the potential to simultaneously reach thousands of learners in schools and communities around the world. The success of e-learning in the developing countries is based on :

(i) existence of an established community of learners

(ii) delivery through a blended face-to-face/electronic mechanism

(iii) offering of learner incentives. All these assume the existence of infrastructure, along with some degree of connectivity. The second requirement for successful implementation of training via e-learning in the developing world concerns the delivery mechanism. Essentially, it is important to use a delivery methodology that combines online instruction i.e., instructor learner interaction, a network of tutors, and off-line course content. The third key factor of a successful e-learning activity in the developing world is the need for an incentive to motivate learners.

Digital Libraries

Information is an intellectual resource that has the capacity to transform the image of society. It has the power of changing the very direction of human life by way of preserving and sharing the essence of knowledge passed down by innumerable wise men to the future generations for posterity and use.

Emergence of ICT, the role of library expands and it is necessary to incorporate technological gadgets and modernize the library services with utmost care and diligence in order to attract the society and justify its existence. Basically they deal with the knowledge and understanding and provide available information to library clients to pursue their interests.

Digital library defined as, "conversion of analog items into digital format for the purpose of extending access and, where appropriate, to assist with preservation. It is a collection of digital objects, including text, video and audio along with methods for access and retrieval, and for selection, organization and maintenance of the collection. Therefore, Digital Library is an organization that provides the resources, including the specialized staff, to select, structure, offer intellectual access to, interpret, distribute, preserve the integrity of, and ensure the persistence over time of collections of digital works so that they are readily and economically available for use by a user's community.

DLs are in fact a connection of complex concepts and technologies which involve different sets of hardware and software technologies which depends on the use and the purpose of the materials to be converted to digitized form.

The library needs digitalization as it is to make available the reading specially rare and fragile materials. This helps to search automatically and swiftly. Preservation of materials is made possible here by making the digital copy available to the readers which saves the original document. Digitization also helps in promoting and marketing of library resources world wide. It increases the revenue of library. Information has got the economic value and also for the sake of society, democracy, education, the advancement of science and technology universally.

A library in which large proportion of the resources are available in machine-readable format and accessible by means of computers. The digital content may be locally held or accessed remotely via computer networks.

The Digital Library is an integration of digital contents and various advanced information technologies built on high performance computing and communication. The fundamental requirements for the digital libraries are process of information selection: selecting libraries, selecting documents, and selecting data.

Digital Library needs to address the important of digitization and include many of the key issues like.

(a) Digital Library Models, frameworks and system requirements

(b) Metadata

(c) System intergration and architecture issues

(d) Interoperability

(e) Networked information discorvery, agent technologies

(f) Information retrieval, organization, navigation-tools and paradigms

(g) Multilinguality

(h) Role of knowledge representation system in DL interactions

(i) Collecting, capturing, filtering, cataloging, indexing.

(j) Preserving

(k) Intellectual property rights, terms and conditions, right management

(l) Authoring, electronic publishing, electronic commerce and information economics

(m) User interfaces, cooperation, and resource sharing.

(n) Scientific models

(o) Digital Library standards

The success of the Digital Library solely lies in its quality and content of the digital resources. It helps in solving many problems like; speedy supply and search of information needs to the library customers with pin pointed and exhaustive in its contents and it enabled to have access remotely and could save lot of space in the library and also it is interoperable. Preservation and space conservation are an added advantage of Digital Library Three are variety of tools like information organization tools, information retrieval tools and collection management tools and techniques are required to build a good information retrieval systems and user interface which leads to building better Digital Library.

Hardware

(a) Computer PIV with high capacity hard disk for server and clients in the LAN, web servers and FTP servers
(b) Workstation PCs
(c) Capture devices-scanners, cameras
(d) High power UPS (10-20kv)
(e) Printers, consoles and test computers
(f) Out put devices CD-ROM, DVD, OCR
(g) High speed LAN, WAN Internet connectivity

Software

(a) Operating software
(b) OCR software
(c) Scanning software
(d) Acrobat reader
(e) CD-Read/Writer software
(f) Digital Library Open Source software e.g. Dspace, Greenstone, Fedora, E-prints etc.
(g) Windows NT networking software, SQL server software, database management software
(h) Web designing software like java, FrontPage, XML etc.
(i) Full text search engine to index and provide access to digital resources.

Metadata

Metadata is "data about data" or information about an image. It's critical to capture as much information about the image in addition to the image itself. Metadata has to be preserved along with the image. Metadata is one of the key aspects for information access in digital libraries.

Digital Library should be able to integrate and aggregate the existing collection and services with an outstanding client interface. This implies that the DL system should have a strong collection interface capable of embracing almost all the popular digital standard and formats and software platforms, inline with the underlying Digital Library technologies in vogue.

Operational tools for digital library

Digital information system's consists of access tools viz. searching, retrieval, locating document, browsing. navigation, archiving digital documents, content delivery, digital preservation, indexing, presentation, extraction, distribution, elicitation, editing, interfacing, online, and so on. There are various operation tools of DL as: e-mail, mailing lists, newsgroups, bulletin boards, web form, polling, instant messaging, chat, conferencing, internet telephony, video conferencing and virtual worlds etc.

Staffing and Training

Digitization needs the dedicated and highly motivated staff. And each of their role must be determined. Staff is also essential to promote the digitization collection. Staff significant activities should also include:

(a) selection coordinator, conservator, curator, or other analysis of the source materials.

(b) Preparation of technician

(c) Scanning technician or photographer.

(d) Quality control technician

(e) Metadata analysis may also be a cataloger.

(f) Data entry technician

(g) Programmer or database technician

(h) System/network administrator.

(i) Web-developer or designer of the user interface.

It is the Digital Library tools and techniques which have impacted the information sharing scenario, through the consortia mode of access, which have undoubtedly increased the information base and opportunity for the research based and potential users, that too at the reduced cost, thereby providing excellent opportunity to maximize the use of information resource.

Many publishers of scientific journals and conference proceeding have started to offer their material over dedicated portals, usually for a subscription fee. A typical example Springer link offers access to more than 1,500 journals, some 700 book series and about 12,000 books with a total of about 3 million documents. Access to titles, abstracts etc. is free, but full papers can only be retrieved through personal or institutional membership. There have been some major public and privately funded digital library projects. It did consider not just textual material at an early stage, but also maps videos etc. A few of the many pointers that are easily found with modern search engines like Google etc.

There is also an increasing amount of grey literature of in various data base system. There is Google Books an attempt to make as many books as possible available online. The i2010 European Digital Library Imitative [i2010 DL 2006] has been announced as major portal.

Material Stored

Digital libraries are now widely available and implemented on different information or document management systems. Material stored in digital libraries is usually organized in some way. Different types of index-pages are usually generated automatically and presented to the user for browsing through the information pace. Articles by author, articles published in an issue or volume, articles by some category, to name just a few different types of indices. The ACM-computing classification schema is often used in computer-science related digital libraries. Modern systems work with a variety of knowledge-management tools to provide some flexibility and tolerance in keyword construction, for example providing typographic error correction or review. It is not possible for a single library to store every single document about a specific are. Thus resources available in external systems must be integrate and reused. A system should provide users with access to content regardless of storage-location. Document content as well as services provided by the remote digital library should be available to users. Unfortunately this portal approach is not commonly used in digital libraries. The portal software should be responsible for distributing search queries to all selected digital libraries and provide search-results to users. This list of results must be presented to the user in a usable and reusable fashion, permitting sorting, emailing, saving and the like. Using a portal-approach for a digital library implicitly leads to many problems, including access rights to content, access to services provided by the remote system, selection of remote systems heading of the results of functions called at the remote system to mention just the most important ones.

Wrapper Software

Access to services provided by digital library is often implemented using wrapper-software. These tools are usually parsers, using regular expressions to access HTML documents (or any other format) and to extract the relevant parts of a result-document. Depending on the wrapper- library used, this approach may fail if the design of the remote-sever hangs. Using XML based remote service invocation will make it easier for the portal-software developer to access remote services.

Interface

Many digital libraries and learning environments adapt the interface to the user. Some of the systems also implement personalization, i.e. adaptation of the content, personalized listings of content, recommendations to content of interest to the use etc. At the moment, users have to express their interest in certain topics via different user interfaces for every system. If interests change, users must change their user-profiles on every system.

In an e-Learning environment the reading-material relating to a certain topic may consist of several resources held by different digital libraries and various e-Learning systems or other web-based systems. This selection of course-material should be automatically gathered together and the resulting collection presented to all members of the course.

Push Service

This is known as alerting service. Many journals use different alert mechanisms to notify registered users. For example, a user may be interested in all newly arrived articles, or articles, matching some query in the full-text, abstract category/classification, or title, or in new articles written by some particular author. Unfortunately, such a feature is presented in different ways by differing systems.

Extended Functions

(a) We take a closer look at the idea of annotations and consider some implications thereafter we explore links, created automatically or manually by uses or a group of users.

(b) Annotations are basically notes attached to documents. First implementations supported just text-based notes. However since annotations are simple objects in a database, it is possible to attach arbitrary multimedia documents as annotations when using a Hyper wave Information Server as database.

In Hyperwave links are stored in a link database in hyperware. It is possible to add links to documents, which do not support links per se.

Hyperwave links even to post script documents, because links re stored in the link-database rather than the document itself. Obviously, it is necessary to use a specially designed viewer to present the links to the user.

Post Script is now superseded by Adobe's Portable Document Format (PDF) where links are specified and viewers are available for many operating systems. Features of PDF include annotation, minor editing, highlighting etc.

Questions may be answered by experienced uses, the author or the expert in the field may answer a question. Questions may also be answered by the system. This concept is called Active Documents. It has shown, that different users ask only a limited set of questions with respect to a screen full of information albeit often with different formulations. Modern knowledge management systems are able to measure similarity between text documents, thus similar questions can be found and presented. If the user is not satisfied with the questions shown, the question may be forwarded to an expert.

Public annotations are visible to every use; therefore the system and the administrator should take care of this feature. Readers should be forced to read certain parts of a document before to being allowed t annotate an article or ask questions about an article. Online user-tracking and user activity-logging are evident pre-requests to implement such features.

Extra-document links are links to other documents stored either on the same server system or stored on a remote server system. The surrounding of a document (i.e. a cluster with similar documents) with documents containing similar concepts or ideas might be visualized via a knowledge map already introduced in many knowledge management systems. A knowledge map with similar articles is easy to create with intro-sever documents because the full-text or an index is available to the system.

Additionally there might be an implementation of links to traditional material. This traditional material (i.e. books or printed journals) is sometimes available at the local library. The local library usually offers a searchable catalogue of available material. Sophisticated systems provide users with status information such as 'the book is currently on loan by another user' or 'the book is available'. Why not reuse this information and integrate it in the listing of reference? Many wrapper-tools are already available to access this kind of information from an online –catalogue system.

e-Learning

Just as traditional libraries support students learning via the content of the library. Learning does not take place simply by accessing content. The information or knowledge must be processed by the learner's mind. Support can be provided in structuring reflecting-analyzing and synthesizing the knowledge, as is evidenced by the numerous so called knowledge management (KM) systems.

Digital library obviously includes content, access to content, and support to 'process' that content, we see further e-Learning functions in need of development.

Such systems should be developed which can provide a wider range of support for learning and teaching, systems that empower, with proven and reliable knowledge Management Systems such as Hyperwave, together with careful consideration of the educational possibilities and imperatives, empowering digital library systems, which support e-learning in the broad sense of the term, are imminent in their realization.

Intelligent Search

Many scholars have experienced that the typical search engines being used to locate information on the Web are not so effective in locating research documents and academic publications accessible via the Internet. There are numerous reasons for this document format-PDF and prost script files are often not indexed by search engines; search scope –the usual scope is WWW. documents and thus does not include scholarly databases or other repositories of published knowledge; idiosyncratic search parameter specification interfaces and search rules; the variety of search interfaces is so large as to create cognitive overload, and of course markedly slow the discovery of relevant documents due to the need for tedious interactions.

'Data, documents books libraries and bigger encyclopedias are available at home after a successful search. However the

Internet is in danger of becoming a labyrinth for the users that have to deal with different interface, with the communication systems of the programmes, so they can end up being confused by the differences that the diverse programmes establish for one operation.'

Major breakthroughs however are going to come once supporting users' diverse mental models or cognitive maps of the knowledge domains being searched by them. The recognition by digital library designers that individual uses' idiosyncratic needs, knowledge or concept maps and search strategies can be supported will result in the cognitive empowerment being sought by scholars the world over.

Visualization of Search Results

Frequency table, star ratings and similar devices are now being used to augment the usual linear lists of search results implied visualization of the information repository's content, which in turn, facilitates more efficient acquisition and retrieval of stored information.

There are methods to represent query results in meaningful ways, among which 'Maps are provided to give a visual overview of the whole document collection with similar documents located close to each other' Repeated fine tuning of search query selection criteria could be contingent upon the graphical output indicating the attainment of a 'suitable' search result density per document, or number of document, and so on.

Some special tools need to be built to support such interactions as that the what if analysis tools provided for example in Microsoft Excel.

Conceptual Searching

Typically we search textual repositories, and use words as the keys to match in the target. Advanced search functions may permit an adjustment of scope, facilitate the use of attribute-fields (e.g. time, authorship subject domain and including the prevalent meta-data tags for WWW material etc.) provide word variant phonetic, or even multi-lingual support. A variety of words can be used to form a concept, and if we want to find concepts as opposed to words we must rethink our search strategy.

When our (key word) searches produce a manageable quantity of results these key-words deliver in respect of our concepts. Such a system works for small to moderate quantities of knowledge. It is unimaginable to even think about the next step, that of using the information found.

'Faculty resist cold ' searching the web for a number of reasons: the thousands of hits returned by search engine queries and the time required to evaluate them; the frequently unrelated or low quality websites returned from a search query; and the many links that are broken or no longer point to relevant material. Therefore information to sort through and high variability of quality of results.'

With key-word searching, we create to represent the search concept. It can not clear whether the search has delivered all (or most) of the potential targets. The system facilitate an interaction between the searcher and that which is being searched. During this interaction, a concept may develop from that of the initial construction into something much more pertinent have mentioned the importance of organizing the information once it is found, and to that end suggest the use of 'concept maps', among other information structuring devices.

White Lists—A portal system is suitable to integrate stored on any other system. In a digital library the concept of white lists, i.e. names or address of systems, which should be integrated in search scopes or any other service, is much more appropriate. It had also been shown in learning environments, that this approach is easier to handle for teachers. Operations in this context are not limited to search operations. One may think also of annotation services, reference analysis, author lists, to mention just a few. Specific White Lists for some readers are not necessarily optimal lists for other readers. Different kinds of lists must exist for different types of readers and for specific topics.

User Interface—User interfaces are needed to provide system functionality to the person wanting to invoke selected functions and should simplify the user's task. There are three different interfaces – a normal version, a light versions.

Software systems can be built to be sensitive to user context, and this is indeed done by most e-commerce sites inter alia through the deployment of Cookies, but usually, or frequently, for purpose other than user type/version, screen resolution, and helper application availability, but the adaptation is rarely dynamic.

There is clearly a need for interaction between the user-interface and a user-interface monitoring agent and also between the user and that agent. User should be able to configure their own interfaces which initially would inherit the design of one of say three main interface options mentioned earlier.

Interface are one of which would be to provide what can be termed session control – much of the work done at computers cannot be completed in one sitting and therefore a system to preserve the workspace or workstage and facilitate a subsequent restart and continuation is directly with the data monitoring by such software.

9

Digital Collection and e-Library

Evolution of Digital Collections

The barriers of space and time in the search for knowledge and also challenged. Today, students, researchers, Information professionals, can directly access many of the world's artifacts right at the desktop or other Web-enabled device, at any time and from any location. Many important advances in digital library techniques came about through research projects these projects began expanding internationally when NSF linked its digital library research program with similar activities being undertaken by JISC U.K., resulting in the JISC-NSF International Digital Library Initiative. Since then, many other groups have become involved in the expansion of digital library technologies and techniques, including the European Union, Association for Computing Machinery (ACM), the Institute of Electrical and Electronics Engineers (IEEE), the International Federation of Library Associations (IFLA), the American Library Association (ALA), the Coalition for Networked Information (CNI), and the Digital Library Federation (DLF).

Definition

It is time to erase the line between physical and digital libraries. "A major portion of library activities are technology-supported and have been for years. The Internet has had an incredible impact, but libraries have a history of managing large systems and using technology to deliver bibliographic information".

Digital library is the electronic extension of functions, users typically perform and the resources they access in a traditional library. These information resources can be translated into digital form, stored in multimedia repositories, and made available through Web-based services.

Objective

Digital libraries began to appear on the campus as research and development projects centred within computer science departments of the librarianities characterizes it as "second-generation digital library" exploring new opportunities and developing new competencies.

Digital libraries can be useful because it-

(a) Gain access to the holdings of libraries worldwide through automated catalogs.

(b) Locate both physical and digitized versions of scholarly articles and books.

(c) Optimize searches, simultaneously search the Internet, commercial database, and library collections.

(d) Save search results and conduct additional processing to narrow or qualify results.

(e) From search results, click through to access the digitized content or locate additional items of Interest.

Components

A fully developed digital library environments involves the following elements:

(a) Initial conversion of content from physical to digital form.

(b) The extraction or creation of metadata or indexing information describing the content to facilitate searching and discovery, as well as administrative and structural metadata to assist in object viewing, management and preservation.

(c) Storage of digital content and metadata in an appropriate multimedia repository.

To interoperate with the existing library infrastructure, the digital library must be designed to work with existing library catalogs and incorporate industry standards, formats, and protocols. Digital library components must also be tailored to capture, encode, and deliver information according to the standard practices adopted by the library industry.

e-Learning and the Campus

The development of digital libraries must be considered in the overall context of initiatives to unify the IT structure of the campus and to transform the learning process through innovative technology. Educational organizations are now viewing themselves in a new light. New types of students and changing student expectations are driving the integration of core campus functions and deployment of student services on the Web. Educators realize the need to link learning and administrative resources in a more effective way to become a "knowledge enterprise".

Clifford Lynch, says – "I think we will see a continued evolution from thinking about digital collections to thinking about networked information services, which will integrate authoring, analysis, and distribution tools that facilitate the reuse and re-purposing of digital content.

Prospects

Digital library technology and its applications has accelerated in recent years as the focus has begun to shift from R&D to full scale deployment. There are new trends emerged as-

(a) The shift from text and image-based systems to audio and video. As network bandwidth becomes more economical and steaming technologies increasing numbers of institutions to access of full multimedia solutions.

(b) Rights management, preservation, metadata encoding, and other key digital library processes.

(c) Providing great reusability for library patrons, increased interoperability among digital collections, and more cost-effective choices for institutions just beginning digitization programs.

(d) Growing dependence on digital information resources will create market pressure for the creation of cooperative solutions for long-term preservation.

(e) Digital libraries will be routinely linked to campus e-learning and administrative systems to provide a one-stop virtual campus.

Instructional Models for Using Weblogs in eLearning

These are students who have grown up in the information age with technology and developed skills, aptitude and attitudes different from many of those active in institution. For example, they look to the internet for information and are comfortable interacting online with their peers; they work collaboratively and thrive on interactivity; and they have an expectation of immediacy not just in problem-solving and knowledge acquisition but from their instructors as well.

Ruth Colvin-Clark and Richard E. Mayer identified three instructional techniques of e-learning:

1. Receptive: information acquisition
2. Directive: response strengthening
3. Guided Discovery: knowledge construction

The receptive technique emphasizes acquiring information and involves building instructional modules that open avenues to greater amounts of information while limiting application and experimentation. In contract to this, the directive technique emphasizes frequent responses from learners with immediate feedback from the instructor. Guided discovery places the instructor in the role of expert who leads students toward solving real-life challenges and identifying the appropriate conceptual codecs to support student knowledge acquisition. Blogging is a simple technology that can be used to construct learning environments that fulfill these three instructional techniques.

The Hybrid Experience

Learning, Reading and Culture are three basis of study. Reading Writing and Text, addressed "readers and writers as users of languages; reading and writing as language processes; and what makes as text a text".

The Blog

Mayer introduced blog as a formative experiment to give students a way to experience so-called "New Literacies" and to help to build a classroom community of learners. It is used for class assignments, reflections, and journal entries. In addition, it served to extend discussions between class meetings and helped in collaborations. Many used it very much for the course activities: literacy inventories, such as lists, purposive reading, observation notes, and linguistic analysis. Students used their blog to chronicle the development of their class projects, which they also regularly presented in chronicle the development of their class projects, which they also regularly presented in class. Sharing information about new technology was at the heart of the Technology News blog. In Technology News, students made direct observations of uses of technology, provided summaries with links to complete articles and added entries relevant to their discipline or personal interests.

Data Type and Format : LongTerm Preservation of Digital Material

Why – Preservation is a response to the threat of destruction some individual must ultimately initiate the response when the threat has been recognized. The reaction may be in a level of value that is placed on the object on the threat. Their reaction incurs a cost which will continue to be incurred, while the threat appears to remain. It needs sufficient funds to meet the cost for the purpose of preservation. Traditional tools and process are insufficient in the modern context. The question arises 'why should this digital material be preserved? Traditional material and sources live short life and it gives threat to their loss. There should be long term viability of any stored information.

(a) What is the rationale for preservation.

(b) When an object is retrieved from the archive, will it be valuable even in 50 years time.

(c) Will the archives will be recognized for a long period.

(d) Research libraries and legal deposit libraries have different requirements when retaining material over long periods of time.

(e) What benefits are measurable?

(f) Who can capture them.

The preservation material is considered to be divided in two categories: (1) material which is not long time valuable (2) the material have a long life of recognition. The archives preserved in sealed capsules must be the material that moves forward technologically in step with the changing world, changing its format and styles and fulfill the purpose. In other words in order to preserve the integrity of digital material, the surrounding medium may need be changed frequently, losing the data in process. The material is scanned recognizing its usability:

(a) What contextual information is necessary for preservation?

(b) Object is to register and indexed and carrying extra information. What contextual information is sufficient and necessary be retrieved and interpreted correctly.

(c) How the object will be accessed and approach to preservation.

(d) In case the object need unchanged and what media is suitable for its storage and upgraded.

The important task is storing, preservation and capturing the material in the archive. There are many complications arise in straightforward process of managing the archive if managers avoid using procedures. There are less risk if procedures are established ignoring human and machine errors.

(a) What are the preservation process and procedural needs in order to achieve a long term archive?

(b) Who are the stakeholders, who manage?

(c) Which are the quick and cost saving routes which are safe for quality?

(d) What safety nets exist?

Technology consists electronic storage used for different purposes. It has different size, security and cost. When and where to preserve dials with the place to create a presence of digital material. The place should be little change overtime.

Components of digital material

The important factors of assessing the complexity of the digital material to be preserved may be enumerated as:

(a) type of material,

(b) type for format,

(c) the current media used to hold the material

(d) the plateform where it is located,

(e) the site where it is to be captured

Complexity lies in every category and analysed by understating or overstating by combined complexity rating:

(a) The preservation cost is high, that the decision is taken the volume of data to be preserved.

(b) There would be infrastructure that database in general and GIS database in particular.

(c) Embedded programs, compression routines, macros and executable code may be hidden and the code is not transferable across technology boundaries.

Score card is to be maintained to assess the quality and time of digital material. It allows cross-referencing and checking of similar cases overtime and across platforms.

The score card will be effected by:

(a) potentiality

(b) simplicity

(c) environment

(d) future expansion

(e) quantity of digital material

(f) the findings of the technology watch

(g) trends in technology diversity

(h) changes in the management

Score cards reflect the principles of frame work and modified as necessary.

Type of Material

(a) ***Textual documents***–They are simple, wellscafed, contained all informations relating to the document within the file. They are simplest items to preserve. Their complexity will low if they use a standard markup language. They are more complex when their nature become of a complex subject. They are macro document and they are intended to work in a network environment and contains HTML linkage.

But there is a risk that the features may not be reproducible or accurately. Either evidential nature of the is diminished, potentially catastrophically. But in later period documents are retrieved without any risk. The loss is restricted to formatting and presentation.

(b) There is a complexity of standards for mapping access and storage.

(c) Features can cause complexity in mark-up of image, sound and video.

Office material to be preserved may be bound together as a book. Their nature is dependent. From the perspective of preservation and future access, the resources that maintain the usefulness of the material are sometimes donated by the software vendors.

Material		Risk
1. Text document (encapsulated)	-	Loss of format
2. Spreadsheets	-	Loss of links
3. Office documents	-	Loss of access to all items
4. Database records	-	Loss of meaning
5. Maps	-	Loss of image quality Ambiguity of platting
6. Image, sound, video	-	Loss of link Loss of meaning Loss of image quality
7. Image database	-	Do not store, recreate

Type of File Format

Other factor effecting the preservation of digital items is the type of file format. Software developers classify the digital items in export and import objects in many different formats. The translation from one to another is not foolproof but it seem the purpose of exchangeability. Many problems arises when:

(a) Item to be preserved is held within a capsule like Microsoft office or Lotus, for displaying.

(b) Translation or display will be the responsibility of the developing software.

(c) Documents in a non-current, non-standard formats cannot be stored in their native format, unless a "Lunch" or "view" mechanism can be stored in a capsule with them.

(d) The text could not be amended during the time the item was in the archive, unless provided a supporting evidence.

Most secure is graphic format to be preserved without any more risk. Each software company adopts standard to suit their product, to limit the problems of upward compatibility, and to enforce custom loyalty.

There are variety of formats in graphic area and the allowable subtypes that exist within them. General category graphics can also not put in one category. Exp. TIFF has many internal formats, all slightly turned for a particular software product or environment. The differences only become apparent when an image is being manipulated compressed or edited.

Format		Risk
1. Standard formats (Recognised)	-	Loss of quality to some extent
2. Standard document-level formats (Recognised)	-	Loss of data
3. Meta and Vector formats (Recognised)	-	Loss of data
4. Graphic formats (Recognised, compressed)	-	Loss of data. May be checked by translation into portable formats
5. Proprietary based formats	-	Loss of data and meaning

The degree of loss in lossy formats is only the concern the purpose for which it was preserved. Loss is an issue for lossy formats when:

(a) through the passage of time

(b) sudden step changes

(c) emerging internet usage popularizes new improved formats

(d) the greater degree of compression leads to a greater degree of "Wobbliness" during processing the image.

Type of Media

Historically the media has not been diversified and storage process is continuously improving for the last 50 years. The important medias are:

1. Tape
2. Disk

Tap: It is most durable device. The original tap storage mechanism have changed size, recording density, encoding, capacity, speed, and reliability.

Disk: Disk is most durable, but the disk has changed more radical than the tap. Optical, Magnato-optical, megnatic and solid state devices now compete to hold commercial data.

There is no choice over the ideal media for long-term preservation of digital material. The media is used either in 8mm DAT volumes or some derivative of CD. The two technologies combine portability, reliability, speed of access and a greater capacity. Because of their qualities, longevity, probability and lack of susceptibility to damage.

Media	Example	Complexity	Risk
Magnetic media (Portable disk)	Diskette	Varient on standards are common. Do not prevent retrieval.	Catastrophic damage
Magno-optical media (Portable disk)	Optical Disk	Obselete in foreseeable future	Lack of data reading device
CD Portable Media (Portable)	WORM (Erasable CD)	Varients in structures and formats	Loss of Access to data
Tape (Portable)	DAT	-do-	Loss of meaning
Network	Disk drives, Tape reels, cartridges, MSS device	Volume and special operational environment	Loss of portability

Operating System

Computer market place is a combination of personal, workgroup, divisional and corporate computing promoted as the answer to business problems. Every new machine have some changes in improved technology to challenge the competition. IBM made a programme through market surveys and introduced a radical new technology. Transparency to the user is declared for every major change in order to alloy fears of another costly transition. The hardware platform is not material as long as the archive media has an operating system – independent file recording and encoding structure. Its file can run on UNIX and Wintal platform. In compatibility can be hidden by product badges, e.g. Windows NT4 supports two file structures: The DOS structure which has a weakvers for fragmentation, and NTFS which is not competible with other windows and DOS formats, because its structure the data on the disk to avoid fragmentation and consequent waste of disk and processor resources. In the same way compatibility of recording material is taken for granted today for CD, audio cassette tapes and videotapes. There are four platforms suitable for the purpose Window NT, SCO-UNIX.

Steps in Preservation Process

Long term preservation service is customer confidence. It is the commitment of stakeholders who entrust unique and possibly priceless material to the archives.

Functions

(a) Overall planning

(b) Reporting

(c) Administration

(d) Access

(e) Retrieval

The archive is a goal for all preserved material and the associated contextual data. It management effect the preservation process. Efficient procedures during archives will not reduce costs during capture, but also further backup the business chain of activities, possibly improving the efficiency of the creator themselves.

(a) ***Policy and Planning***: Technology trends take 2-3 years to unfold. Technology watch also permits more detailed transition planning to be made for the archives configuration.

(b) ***Administration Management***: The archive will have all the requirements of a small business to manage its assets draw on local expertise and report back to branch management on the day to day practicability and trends.

(c) ***Preservation Engineering***: It is a preliminary work and differentiate the evidented and waste material. Some ephemeral material may be duplicate or not required, in which case a photograph would satisfy the record. The material is processed through:

(i) Media conversion

(ii) Format conversion

(iii) Material conversion

(iv) Processing conversion

10

e-Book and e-Library

At Every book, we are pursuing a vision of how publishers, readers, and the environment can benefit from an electronic book system that does not compromise the very things we love about books. It involves two guiding principles:

(1) A book is information, but information is not necessarily a book. Books do not create themselves out of a pile of information. A guiding hand must economically and profitably find and nurture authors. It must catalog and edit manuscripts, check facts, and shepherd words and ideas through a written journey from introduction to conclusion. It must oversee production, promotion, and distribution in a way that apportions revenue and protects future sales. The Internet cannot perform these functions. A traditional bookstore or library cannot complete all of these tasks.

(2) What a computer does best, a book cannot do; and what a book does best, a computer cannot. Computers work well in document creation, editing, storage, and distribution. But a fully functional computer cannot bring its display any closer to your eyes than the length of your bent arms because of its pointing device or keyboard.

Books transport and display knowledge and feelings in a comfortable, familiar format. Books have no learning curve for usage. They display a huge amount of textual and graphical information for their weight, cost, and size. Our hands balance them perfectly, paginating without the loss of context or theme treats-books as bulky and unwieldy pieces of machinery. They are kept somewhere that the reader has to visit in order to use.

The Evolution of the Page and Book

The Sumerian tablet represents the oldest example of human textural writing. The tablet gave way to the scroll for the obvious reasons of greater storage capacity with less weight.

The scroll ultimately became the codex, or modern book. In the past two centuries, books have standardized around two basic sizes: reference, in a roughly 8.5”×11” configuration; and entertainment, in a 5.75”×8.5” design. These sizes maximize paper production with the least amount of waste.

Publisher

The evolution of the page and book took place in the age of the manuscript. The manuscript age did not involve printing, publishing or cataloging. Even after the rise of the merchant class and the early university system of the 12th and 13th centuries, learning was dependent on the manual production of individual manuscripts.

The universities, which created a demand for books, relied on stationers for paper, and book copiers to supply students with commissioned duplications. Stationers had no way of knowing the accuracy of copies of the texts, which were often brought back by the crusaders from the Moors who collected them from Egypt, Greece and Palestine. So the rise of the university created a demand, but the technology of the time and the lack of publishers and a business model shifted it as well.

In the mid 15th century, Gutenberg brought together the technologies of moveable type, paper, oil-based ink and the wine-press to more efficiently print books. The advent of the printing press, however, did not bring about a great shift in the social organization of learning in Europe. Many people went into the printing business and went right back out again because the distribution of books was poorly organized. The market was there, and the potential for filling the demand, but the transport, control, and "advertising" mechanisms were not in place. But is modern age.

Unlike television and film, however, the web appears to be delivering on its promise to reshape learning, although at a much slower pace than previously anticipated. And libraries are poised to support web-based e-learning by creating and managing e-content, developing new services and linking their current ones to course management systems, the hub for e-teaching and e-learning. E-learning and e-content represent a golden opportunity for libraries to expand their role in the digital age. Electronic elements are changing the way faculty and students access, create and use information, and libraries can play a role in helping their communities effective combine content and technology."

The emergence of a network culture and the digital student are among the factors driving the rapid growth of web-based, e-learning, weather it's course taught online over a distance or traditional courses that have been enhanced with electronic elements. And e-learning's convenience, reach and novel pedagogical resources can potentially improve education by providing high quality, customized instructions to the greatest number of people.

E-content V/s E-learning

E-content is the heart of e-learning. Online articles, streaming video, audio segments, images, specially designed web sites and unique learning objects are electronic elements which are created to enhance courses and improve learning. They may be selected segments from a larger information resource, such as an video clip, or a custom-made object designed by a faculty member, such as an animated map that shows how national boundaries have changed over time. They engage today's computer-savvy student, whose learning style more interactive, having been raised with computers, the Internet and video games.

While electronic books and texts have been available for some time for selected public domain titles, only relatively recently have electronic texts been packaged and offered commercially as electronic books. It is the shift to the commercial production, sale, and distribution of e-books that has changed how libraries need to deal with e-books, and what prompted our investigation. Electronic books offer creative possibilities for expanding access as well as changing learning behavior and academic research. Content can always be accessible, regardless of time or place, to be read on PCs or on portable bouk readers. Books need never go out of print, and new editions can be easily created. One can carry several titles at once on a portable reader and, over time, build a personal library. Features such as full text searching, changeable font size, mar-up, citation creation, and note taking will enhance usability. Print text can be integrated with multi-dimensional objects, sound, and film to create a whole new kind of monographic work.

Use of e-books in academic use-

(a) Content
(b) Software Standards
(c) ·Hardware Standards
(d) Digital Rights Management
(e) Access
(f) Archiving
(g) Privacy
(h) The Market and Pricing
(i) Enhancements and Ideal E-Book Features

Content

Although there are vendors such as Questia, netLibrary, Ebrary and publisher initiatives that are aggressively building undergraduate e-book collections, the corpus of academic level e-books available is still small and not yet representative of many disciplines. Collection building, so far, is hampered by publishers conservatism in providing rights to title for e-book distribution and venders costs to reformat content from proprietary versions. At the academic level, subject areas with a broader customer base, such as computer science, business, and reference, are growing most rapidly.

Academic researchers need to rely on authenticity and integrity of content. E-book content should match any print version and include all its elements: text, graphs, and illustrations. Content needs to be separated from access and manipulation features, and needs to be transferable, in non-proprietary format, into a variety of software and hardware readers, both to offer readers a choice of additional features, and to make it possible for libraries to loan e-book content.

Software Standards

Non-commercial monographic electronic texts for scholarly exchange have been available on the Internet since the early years of UNIX file exchange, file transfer (FTP), gopher and, finally, hypertext transfer (HTTP) protocols. The presentation and use of electronic texts have been based on the capabilities and limitations of personal workstation hardware equipped with freely available web browsers and browser plugins.

Currently, there is no established standard for an interoperable e-book format for commercially produced e-books that addresses publishers needs to support commercial end-user distribution and that also enables added value for the consumer. At this point, although publishers are creating books electronically, more often than not text is created in a proprietary from that requires reformatting or scanning of the print version for adaptation to an individual vender's system. Of the current formats, large vendors are using HTML, XML or PDF as defaults. To serve a large and varied academic clientele and to build a strong scholarly collection for long-term access, electronic books must be provided in a standards-based format that includes:

(a) Non-proprietary software and hardware for interoperability of files

(b) Identifiers

(c) Metadata

(d) ADA compliance

The most promising standards are being developed by the Open E-book Forum (OEB) as the Open eBook Publication

Structure, which would ensure interoperability with both PC and portable reading devices. The structure will include metadata, identifiers, and a file structure for both software and hardware so that publishers can provide content without having to reformat it for each reading system. Although the current framework does not yet account for recognize the potential increase in unconventional multimedia integration with text, its elements of interoperability would make a significant step in the viability of e-books. Another element needed in the structure is the element of non-proprietary usability of content, which would allow sharing or loaning information.

Hardware Standards

It makes the reading and using more easier. Yet e-books hardware devices are still not quite practical, they are cost effective enough to penetrate very deploy into the market. A variety of devices are being developed to replicate some of the virtues of printed monographs, including portability and network-independence, so that e-books themselves will function on a variety of platforms. There are two kinds of e-books readers (1) Full size readers (2) Palm sized readers. Currently, both readers use proprietary file formats.

Digital Rights Management

The main element in the development of electronic publishing involves digital rights management systems (DRMS). DRMS which is in developing stage are either hardware or software (or both) that enforce control over intellectual property, such as limit by user, time, fee, and/or extent of content. Although similar controls have existed in the licensing of electronic journals, the length of book content and the concerted effort by publishers to establish such software for e-books make this issue more pressing. Due to publishers concerns about rights, to date e-book venders are normally able to offer only limited usage rights for printing, downloading and copying. Normally, interlibrary loan is not allowed, and classroom use is also not allowed always.

The degree of control e-book publishers choose to exercise over the access, sharing and loaning of intellectual property will make e-books either more or less compatible with the free flow of information needed in the scholarly setting. To support open research, libraries will need "ownership" or "first sale" rights that allow perpetual access and fair use, such as classroom use and the ability to loan the textual content to other libraries. It will not be feasible to create a print copy of entire monographs for interlibrary loan, as is done for journal articles.

Major DRMS (Digital rights Management System) developments are as under-

- ONIX, a book industry standard for communicating product information, including DRMS.
- Adobe Acrobat Web Buy (ACWB) controlling access to PDF documents.
- XrML, a joint effort of Xerox and Microsoft.
- Open Digital Rights Language (ODRL), a project of the World Wide Web Consortium (W3C).

Access

Libraries must be able to integrate titles with other formats in catalogs and integrated library systems, in standardized forms of bibliographic information and in metadata, such as MARC records and other appropriate metadata. Standardized identifiers and metadata will also be necessary to integrate e-books into normal workflows of integrated library systems for functions such as order, payment, cataloging and circulation. Vender-supplied metadata should also be able to accept open URL queries.

Currently, vendors working with libraries use a one-copy-one user model following a traditional print monograph purchase model. Depending on the type of information being purchased, a single user may not be using the entire book text, but only querying a potion of it. A single chapter in an edited work may be what is needed, rather that the entire volume. Ways it accommodates partial book use by simultaneous users need to be factored into licensing.

Archiving and Long Term Access

There are two roles of academic libraries building research level (a) Collection (b) Acting, as archives of research information. Currently, e-book vendor purchase models allow some flexibility, such as a premium price for perpetual access (and potential archiving) versus more modest pricing for annual access to a revolving group of titles. The ability to manipulate an e-book collection easily to eliminate older editions is attractive where currency matters. In order disciplines where long-term research is essential, assurance of perpetual access will be vital.

The Market and Pricing

There are only a handful of Vendors, such as net Library, that offer-books to libraries-particularly with academic content. Publishers have been conservative in moving into the e-book market, and direct publisher offerings are only recently beginning to appear. The viability if e-book vendors are also still uncertain. Since the task Force investigations began, two vendors delayed start-up (one is still not operation), one vendor has discontinued its product, and another stopped accepting new library subscriptions. Vendors offer an array of business modals for e-book selection, including:

(a) Print on demand
(b) Flat monthly subscription to a vendor's complete database
(c) Free browsing of a vendor's database with fees for printing and downloading
(d) Personalization (creation of one's own document by selecting segments/chapters from several sources)

The demand for simultaneous access to individual e-book titles should not require libraries to purchase multiple copies of e-books, and pricing models should be developed that permit some level of simultaneous access. It is suggested one possible pricing model with access fees to allow simultaneous access of a single title, through floating "tokens", very similar to the pooled ports for other databases. The numbers of tokens would be negotiated to represent, for example, at least one single use for every title purchased in a particular database or system. Such tokens would allow a specified number of users for a particular set of e-books regardless of which titles are being accessed simultaneously, but it would not exceed the total number of tokens allowed for that database or system.

The function of e-book varied as inclusion of multi-media information, full text searching, mark-up, citation formatting, reference linking, convenience, portability, interoperability on a variety of devices, availability in advance of print, advantageous pricing, and the ability to share or loan information,,. Given the variety of user needs, nor-proprietary interoperability of e-book content will be needed.

Academic Institutions and E-books

Institutions are still in the trial stage with e-books, and the institutions are still tentative about development of future collections.

(a) Acquisition of e-books has had little or no impact on their purchase of titles in print. Some commented that they felt the role of e-books was not to replace print but to serve s a duplicate copy.

(b) Most institution obtained the MARC records directly from the vendor or through OCLC and added links for electronic versions. Institutions not queried cataloged free e-books resources.

(c) Link and Website are common factors used for publicity method. Other ways included writing articles for faculty or campus newsletters; creating flyers; sending targeted emails; and including e-books in bibliographic instruction.

(d) Mostly institutes how not used feedback mechanisms. Some had anecdotal evidence that users liked having online access, especially the 24x7 aspect.

(e) Most libraries has not purchased portable reading devices;

(f) Respondents generally not express concern about interlibrary loan.

The role of e-books in academic libraries is still not clear, and there is considerable development of standards, technologies, and pricing models needed to make the market for e-books viable and sustainable. Technologies for reading and using e-books are not yet convenient enough for the longer text format to have made much market penetration It is not clear that academic libraries can replace print with e-books as a long term collection goal. There are still concerns about adequate rights to information to support the academic mission of open scholarly communication.

Print Media Journal

Textbooks are a ubiquitous part of student life. Student must carry these heavy, unwieldy textbooks to and from class, home, and the library on a daily basis. Students spend hours pouring over detailed concepts and thousands of pages of materials over the course of their education. Walking around a college campus, the evidence of new technology is everywhere.

(1) The cost of a semester's worth of nooks and the weight of carrying them back to the dorm room. Many textbooks cost more than 500. An Indian students hardly purchase 3-4 books a year on average. College textbooks are a huge business with a steady demand from year to year. Even high school students, book-bags are becoming heavier as they increasingly bring multiple textbooks home to study. As a mature industry, the textbook market presents an excellent opportunity for introducing new technologies, including electronic textbooks.

Reading electronic books currently involves using a PC or laptop computer. Electronic materials on computers usually don't have the functionality of a traditional textbook. And given that PCs aren't portable, the only way to bring an electronic book on computer to class or the library would be on a laptop. Students have learned to study in a particular manner and offering them the benefits of electronic content without asking them to change the way they study is very important.

(2) ***Course Material***: Another option is to provide course materials on handheld devices, such as Page Digital Age, which

generally are considered too small to be conducive for studying, or electronic book readers. There are many additional benefits that can be leveraged in electronic texts. Think about incorporation animation to graphically illustrate the experiments a student reads about in a chemistry book. While there are several excellent handheld e-book readers on- the market, most are designed for trade books and target a general consumer audience without providing multimedia capabilities that will take textbooks to the next level.

Responding to market opportunity, goReader became the first e-book company to offer electronic content on a portable device specifically designed for the education market. At present, goReader is the only wireless electronic reader to offer students at every level the functionality of traditional textbooks and electronic content coupled with the benefits of an Internet appliance.

Inquiry Based Learning

Inquiry implies involvement that leads to understanding. Furthermore, involvement in learning implies possessing skills and attitudes that permit you to seek resolutions to questions and issues while you construct new knowledge. "Inquiry" is defined as "a seeking for truth, information, or knowledge—seeking information by questioning." Individuals carry on the process of inquiry from the time they are born until they die. This is true even though they might not reflect upon the process. Infants begin to make sense to the world be inquiring. From birth, babies observe faces that come near, they grasp objects, they put things in their mouths, and they turn toward voices. The process of inquiring begins with gathering information and data through applying the human senses –seeing, hearing, touching, tasting, and smelling.

Unfortunately, our traditional educational system has worked in a way that discourages the natural process of inquiry. Students become less prone to ask questions as they move through the grade levels. In traditional schools, students learn not to ask too many questions, Instead to listen and repeat the expected answers.

Some of the discouragement of our natural inquiry process may come from a lack of understanding about the deeper nature of inquiry-based learning. There is even a tendency to view it as " fluff" learning. Effective inquiry is more than just asking questions. A complex process is involved when individuals attempt to convert information and data into useful knowledge. Useful application of inquiry learning involves several factors: a context for questions, a framework for questions, a focus for questions, and different levels of questions. Well-designed inquiry learning produces knowledge formation that can be widely applied.

Iinformation is not the most important sill in today's world. Facts change, and information is readily available –what's needed is an understanding of how to get and make sense of the mass of data.

Educators must understand that schools need to go beyond data and information accumulation and move toward the generation of useful and applicable knowledge... a process supported by inquiry learning. In the past, our country's success depended on our supply of natural resources. Today, it depends upon a workforce that "works smarter."

Through the process of inquiry, individuals construct much of their understanding of the natural and human-designed worlds. Inquiry implies a "need or want to know" premise. Inquiry is not so much seeking the right answer—because often there is non but rather seeking appropriate resolutions to questions and issues. For educators, inquiry implies emphasis on the development of inquiry skills and the nurturing if inquiring attitudes or habits if mind that will enable individuals to continue the quest for knowledge throughout life.

Content of disciplines is very important, but as a means to an end, not as an end in itself. The knowledge base for disciplines is constantly expanding and changing. No one can ever learn everything. But everyone can better develop their skills and nurture the inquiring attitudes necessary to continue the generation and examination of knowledge throughout their lives. For modern education, the skills and the ability to continue learning should be the most important outcomes.

Human society and individuals within society constantly generate and transmit this fund of knowledge. Experts, working at the boundary between the known and the unknown, constantly add to the fund of knowledge. It is very important that knowledge be transmitted to all the members of society, This transmission takes place through structures like schools, families, and training courses.

Certain attributes are necessary for both generating and effectively transmitting the field of knowledge. The attributes that experts use to generate new knowledge are very similar to the qualities essential for the effective transmission of knowledge with in the learner's environment. These are the essential elements of effective inquiry learning:

(a) Experts see patterns and meanings.

(b) Experts have in depth knowledge of their fields, structured so that it is most useful.

(c) Experts, knowledge is not just a set of facts-it is structured to be accessible, transferable, and applicable to a variety of situations.

(d) Experts can easily retrieve their knowledge and learn new information in their fields with little effort.

Inquiry is important in the generation and transmission of knowledge. It is also an essential for education, because the fund of knowledge is constantly increasing. The figure below illustrates why trying to transmit "what we know," even if it were possible, is counterproductive in the long run. This is why schools must change from a focus on "what we know " to an emphasis on "how we come to know."

An effective and well-rounded education gives individuals very different but interrelated views of the world. All disciplines have important relationships that provide and natural and effective framework for the organization of the school curriculum. The subject matter of disciplines can be set in the larger context of a **conceptual framework.** This framework is crucial for understanding change and also for the organization of the discipline and its application to the natural and human –designed worlds.

An important out come of inquiry should be useful knowledge about the natural and human-design -worlds. How are these worlds **organized**? How do they **change**? How do they **interrelate?** And how do we communicate about, with in and cross these worlds? These broad concepts contain important issues and questions that individuals will face throughput their lives. Also, these concepts can help organize the content of the school curriculum to provide a relevant and cumulative framework for effective learning. An appropriate education should provide individuals with different ways of viewing the world, communication about it, and successfully coping with the questions and issues of daily living.

While questioning and searching for answers are extremely important parts of inquiry, effectively generating knowledge from this questioning and searching is greatly aided by a conceptual context for ultimate outcome of learning, neither should they be asking questions and searching for answers about minuteness. Well –designed inquiry-learning activities and interactions should be set in a conceptual context so as to help students accommodate knowledge as they progress from grade to grade. Inquiry in education should be about a greater understanding of the world in which they live, learn, communicate and work.

There are several variations on inquiry-based learning. Among the most widely used are the **Future Problem Solving Program** and the **Problem-based Learning Approach.** See the "Resources" section for more on these approaches.

The habits of mind, values, or "group rules" of a particular discipline provide that discipline's unique perspective. The sciences, for example, demand verification of data, while the study of literature often relies on opinions and subjective interpretations as a source of information. Habits of mind vary in their rigidity across disciplines. This doesn't mean that one is right and the other is wrong, but simply that the "ground rules" are different.

11
Electronic Publishing

Electronic publishing includes the digital publication of e-books and electronic articles, and the development of digital libraries. Electronic publishing has become common in scientific publishing where it has been argued that peer-reviewed paper scientific journals are in the process of being replaced by electronic publishing. Although network distribution is now-a-days strongly associated with electronic publishing, there are many non network electronic publications relied on by mobile users and others without reliable and high speed access to a network.

Electronic publishers are able to provide quick gratification for late-night readers, books that customers might not be able to find in standard book retailers (erotica is especially popular in e-Book format) and books by new authors that would be unlikely to be profitable for traditional publishers. Hyponymis are Online publishing, ePublishing, Web Publishing. While the term "Electronic Publishing" is primarily used today to refer to the current offerings of online and web-based publishers, the term has a history of being used to describe the development of new forms of production, distribution, and user interaction in regards to computer-based production of text and other interactive media.

ACJ Net: Electronic Publishing

Definitions

The network of networks, the Internet, permits all of this opinion to contradict each other, to be linked to each other, to appear unrelated, and to repeat itself–to free-associate. Most of the sources for this review of electronic publishing are those who have been involved with traditional publishing, so the voice of those who advocate that messages in e-mail, newsgroups or websites are part of electronic publishing are not as loud.

"Electronic devices in all aspects of the production, management, and distribution of data to users" to the broad domain of all things "viewed, navigated, annotated, and distributed via CD-ROM, over a network, or through on-line service".

While Russell (1996) makes a distinction between electronic publishing and websites or homepages and include them in the range of electronic publishing activities, referring to new search features, valuable hotlinks, meta-sites, newsgroups, and discussion list archives.

Grolier's Electronic Encyclopedia

"Sometimes used to describe the application of computers to traditional print publishing – from word processing to computerized order processing – the term electronic publishing refers more precisely to the storage and retrieval of information through electronic communications media. It can employ a variety of formats and technologies, some already in widespread use by businesses and general consumers, and others still being developed Electronic publishing technologies can be classified into two general categories, those in which information is stored in a centralized computer source and delivered to the user by a telecommunication system and those in which the data is digitally stored on a disk or other physically deliverable medium. The former category, including online database services and videotext, represents the most active area in electronic publishing today".

The dynamic features of the web are exploited in the most successful electronic publications. As in any good educational materials, the elements of electronic publishing include audience specifications, purpose statement, objectives, an overview of the information contained, the technical range and constraints of the publication, and its presentation mechanics. The standard elements of instructional design guide the production of these elements:

planning, analysis, design, implementation, and evaluation and revision. Promotion is introduced as an important process, targeting general Web audiences, potential users and current users, to connect users with needs.

Issues in Electronic Publishing

Electronic publishing can occur outside the realm of the Internet, others agree that mastery of electronic publishing means mastery of tools, practices, and production on the Internet. In order to exist, electronic publishing needs authors who want to publish electronically, people with skills to produce electronic text, media which will enable dissemination of electronic format material, standards which are common, agreed upon, accessible, powerful and cheap, users with the technology to use electronic text, and technology powerful enough to provide an infrastructure.

Technical barriers may limit the scope and impact of electronic publishing. Not all features of an electronic publication can necessarily be accessed by all users. On the other hand, if developers reach for the lowest common denominator, the results may be boring and ignored, or avoided by high end users. The Web, however, is not the whole network and use of facilities, like gopher, file transfer protocol (ftp), and e-mail, may alleviate some of the limitations for some users.

Designing Electronic Documents for the WWW

Producing electronic publications requires some modification to writers' and developers' skills. Some of the key elements need to be logical introductory indexes, precise, concise writing, easily scanned, and written in inverted pyramid style (cf. newspaper articles), accurate spelling and grammar, avoidance of, limited graphics (including smaller logos), proof-read and field-tested applications, limits on hyperlinks, short pages, well-labelled (author, date) with links to home page, quick response time on e-mailed inquiries, a search facility, membership appeal and capture, and regular revisions and updates (Powers, 1997 and Nielsen, 1997).

E-Publishing and Communication

Publishing sets the relationship between the generator (author) and its clientele. Thereby bridging the gap between the author and the distribution mechanism to reach the end user. With the onset of electronic publication, which has now become the most important value-added service that a publisher performs electronic medium is changing relationships and functions in whole research publication cycle. There are three revolutions: language; writing Printing Technology and Internet – Web and Electronic Publishing which has lasting impact on all the key players. The technology allows publishers to get information to readers quickly and with value addition, it is causing major changes to the publishing industry.

E-Publishing or electronic publishing is the distribution of information, art or software, delivered electronically via internet, CD-ROM, or other electronic devices. This material could be in the form of journals, books, music, information sites, reports etc. It allows us almost immediate access to information – anytime, anywhere. New hardware and software offerings are being developed continually, providing even more and diverse ways to deliver and receive content. Electronic publishing is developing on practical, theoretical, and technological fronts simultaneously. E-publishing is a very broad term that manifesting itself in wide range of products and services encompasses a variety of different publishing models and delivery methods, including electronic journals (e-journals), electronic books (e-books), print-on-demand (POD), email publishing, wireless publishing, electronic ink and web publishing.

E-journals and E-books are electronic versions of journals and books which are delivered to consumers in digital formats.

There are a large number of devices being developed to make reading e-books easier for consumers. This market could develop faster than expected because leading publishers and technology companies are pouring money resources into e-book technology.

Any journal, magazine, e-zine, webzine, newsletter or type of electronic serial publication which is available over the Internet can be accessed using different technologies i.e. WWW, Gopher, ftp, telnet, e-mail or listserv. While e-Books are portable hardware and software system that can display large quantity of readable textual information to the user.

An institutional repository or e-print archive is a digital repository of the research output of an institution that is usually accessible freely to end-users both within and outside of the institution. Alternative publishing models and solutions are being evolved. Distributed, inter-operable e-print repositories are emerging as a new publishing model. Institutional E-Print Archives – could have refereed research literature online through author/institution self-archiving that may include Pre-prints, Post-prints (refereed papers), Departmental working papers, lecture series, Conference papers, Theses, Magazine articles, book chapters, etc. Print-on-Demand is a new method for printing the content which allows printing on demand or one copy at a time. The technology involves complex laser printing systems and electronically formatted text which the printers can read. Since this involves print version also, it may not find a niche in the long run. Print-on-Demand players: Barnes & Noble, NetLibrary, IBM, Xerox, Lightening, Sprout, Xlibris, Borders.com, etc.

Media Types and File Formats

Important media types are CD-ROM, DVD-ROM; Networked; Web-based (Intranet or Internet).

Format is used to store and save a file is called a file format. Used typically while referring to a graphical file such as GIF, JPEG, or PNG. The patterns and standards used to store a program on a disk. Examples are GIF, JPEG, TIFF. Contents include text, data, spreadsheet, database, power point presentation (ppt), graphics, audio, video; executable programs: Client Server sides.

There are Formats and Encoding used for text are (a) Simple Text or ASCII; (b) Structured Text Format: SGML; HTML, XML, (c) Page Description Language (PDL) – Adobe's PostScript and PDF (Portable Document Format); (d) Page Image Format – TIFF

(Tagged Image File Format), GIF (Graphical Interchange Format) & JPEG (Joint Photographer's Expert Group).

Standardized General Markup Language (SGML) – It is not a single language but a framework for defining particular markup languages. It is effective solution for handling complexity of electronic publishing. Unlike HTML, SGML does not have proprietary codes. An SGML document consists of three distinct parts namely: (i) Declaration – gives fundamental information like language of document and code set being used (i.e. English/ASCII) (ii) DTD – details of codes and rules restricting their use, and (iii) Instance – the text being published, marked up with the codes described in the DTD. SGML is all about structural and contents and not appearance and display. Besides, SGML-coded documents can be used to search information contents of documents based on the structure and content and documents can move from system to system.

Extensible Markup Language – A subset of SGML, its files are consistent and compatible with SGML. It also deals with Structure and Contents of Document and not its appearance and formatting. The Cascading Style Sheet (CSS), developed for HTML, is used to take care of formatting and appearance. Unlike HTML, XML allows for the invention of new codes. While SGML allows "tag minimization", enabling the omission of end tags, XML always requires explicit end tags that make it a lot easier to write tools and browsers. XML document can be re-formatted in into RTF, LaTeX or any other format using XSL (Extensible Style Language). Like SGML, it offers database functionality and XML codes can be validated by parsing XML file with its DTD, but DTD is not a necessity in XML. The boundaries of every part of a document, whether it is a new chapter, a piece of text, or a reference to another publication are clearly identified. The structure of a document can be checked if the user provides a document type definition that declares each of the permitted entities, elements and attributes, and the relationships between them.

Hypertext Markup Language (HTML)–HTML can incorporate text, graphics, images in a decent layout. Web browser readily accommodate a multitude of plug-ins that allow inclusion of audio, video, 3-D, and other specialized files and it can be imbedded as a link in a standard HTML page. HTML files are tiny since they are simple text files, because of the simplicity of HTML is also its serious limitation for Complex text like books and journals. HTML web pages can be transformed into vibrant, dynamic and interactive web creations using ever evolving web technologies like CGI Script, Perl, Java, JavaScript, ASP, DHML, XML and open database connectivity (ODBC) for incorporating interactivity on a web site. The only contents that it describes are in Metadata codes or in its title. An HTML file can be derived from an SGML file any time but the reverse is not possible.

Page Description Language (PDL) – Page Description Languages confine themselves to describe and define page layout and appearance of a document. PostScript and PDF are two most used Page Description Languages.

Portable Document Format (PDF) – Portable Document Format or Print the Damn File (PDF) is a by-product of PostScript, for page integrity & layout of page. PDF is a proprietary item which browser cannot read on its own. A PDF file is a self-contained cross-platform document and can be viewed across multiple platforms using the appropriate reader; PDF files are page independent, i.e. a user can extract any given page for printing. PDF files preserves all of the fonts, formatting, colors, and graphics of any source document, regardless of the application and platform used to create it or the platform or device. PDF files are compact and can be shared, viewed, navigated, and printed exactly as intended by anyone with a free Adobe Acrobat Reader.

E-publishing transforms raw manuscript into printed artifacts. The process of publishing and transition from print to electronic involves several steps.

1. Call for paper
2. Preparation of manuscript / submission of papers
3. Proof reading / editing / refinement
4. Peer review /refereeing

5. Revision
6. Layout / presentation
7. Publication
8. Binding / distribution
9. Marketing.

Electronic distribution of digital documents can definitely reduce the cost. Publisher's overhead cost is common for both paper and for support activities like editorial work, sales. The cost of printing and distribution of publications is modest of the overall cost on journal publishing. Expenditures in the Process of Electronic Publishing could be (a) publisher's revenue per article; (b) libraries processing cost; (c) editorial and refereeing cost; (d) author's cost for preparing the paper.

Electronic publishing not only bringing down the cost of publishing but also the library cost. Factors that would help cut-down the cost of journal publishing are – (a) advances in technology, (b) scholars function.

There are two types of opinions: (a) Self-Publishing (b) Commercial Publishing.

(a) **Self-Publishing**: It mean that the creator as an independent entity is/are responsible for all aspects of production, marketing and distribution of your product (book, etc.). In exchange for taking on these responsibilities and costs, one will have complete control over the product and the profit it generates, if applicable.

(b) **Commercial Publishing** – Commercial publishers facilitating multipronged access to their e-resources and across other digital data repositories. There are two option to it:

(i) Academic Market – Supply of and demand for articles determined by current research and the quality of output.

(ii) Commercial Market relatively conventional market with publishers providing a product to Libraries.

Methods—Therefore broadly the e-publishing methods would include:

(a) commercial access-controlled publishing
(b) commercial open access publishing
(c) open access repositories

Open access encourages wider use of information assets. Availability of electronic format is leading to changes in business relationships between authors and publishers, between publishers and agents between publishers and librarians and between publishers and readers.

Author's changes

(a) **Author-driven initiatives** – There are two school of thoughts – Open access archives (e-prints archives) and open access journals. Influencing commercial publishers by bringing out open access journals with an aim to use author-power to make commercial publications freely available.

(b) **Commercially-driven initiatives** – It facilitates immediate free access to peer-reviewed research using new model to cover publication costs. New aggregation services-one-stop shop for varied content and new e-book companies aiming to change business models and access routes to monograph literature.

(c) **Collaborative initiatives** – That are creating change and declaring independence which has raised awareness of scholarly communication issues in many academic institutions. It is facilitating access to scholarly journal contains at low cost through various approaches.

The e-publishing is a reality of the present and a definite go better for the future. However, the future of e-publishing would greatly depend on user's perception.

Usage—The usage both in terms of direct and indirect may be useful, where indirect here means graph or trend of subscribing to e-resources, while the direct means the actual usage of these e-resources by the potential users.

(a) Organisations are maintaining spend on e-resources and in many cases adding to this component of their library budget. Besides they are trying to tap various others forms of resources.

(b) Many organizations are realizing the importance of access to information on touch of button. Many have showed up there interest and are opting for e-alternatives as well. During the last few years there has been a definite growth and realization of access to e-resources all over the world.

There is a rapid evolution in scholarly communication. Usage is moving to electronic formats. In some areas, it appears that electronic versions of papers are being read about as often as the printed journal versions. The growth rates in usage of electronic scholarly information are sufficiently high that if they continue for a few years, there will be no doubt that print versions will be eclipsed. Further, much of the electronic information that is accessed is outside the formal scholarly publication process. There is also vigorous growth in forms of electronic communication that take advantage of the unique capabilities of the web.

New Publishing Paradigm

INSA is a signatory to the Berlin Declaration on open access. We explored its usage as a repository and as a publishing distribution platform for low-cost open access publishing that encompasses all disciplines and is openly accessible worldwide. At the same time to exploit attributes of online publishing that were not feasible with a paper-based model for bridging the digital divide and create facilities for digital provide or opportunities. The e-publishing activities though primarily focus on the scholarly literature published in scientific journals, but creation of other types of digital repositories have also been attempted which will also receive some attention here.

INSA

In the area of e-publishing activities, INSA (Indian National Science Academy) took several initiatives and created e-journals and other e-repositories. It was with this motive that electronic publishing of journals together with creation of open access institutional repositories buttressed the e-publishing activities at INSA. These eventually blossomed into E-Scholarship@insa - a timely convergence of institutional repository, e-journal initiatives, and other digital publishing projects.

INSA brings out several research journals, that includes Indian Journal of Pure & Applied Mathematics [IJPAM] (1970); Proceedings of the National Institute of Sciences of India (1935-55); Proceedings of the National Institute of Sciences of India Pt A [Physical Sciences] (1955-2006); Proceedings of the Indian National Science Academy (March 2006-) and Indian Journal of History of Science (1966-).

Purpose

(a) To improve the process of scientific communication by applying new technologies.

(b) Provide and support concept of free Access to scientific literature.

(c) Building up of a national resource base with global visibility and accessibility.

e-journal portal was launched formally for public use in December 2002 having almost 70 year archives for all the scholarly publications of the scholarly publications, where the leading international experts and promoters of open access to scientific literature participated.

Features:

(a) **Free Access**: The digitization of all the journals has been carried out right from the first volume. The retro conversion activity was completed in beginning of 2002 and made available online since 2002-03. All the journals are web accessible for free, unlimited and unrestricted access. http://www.insa.ac.in.

(b) **Registration**: Registration is free one time process and will provide personal login details (username and password), which will allow to read the articles/

publications presented online. All the articles are available in the pdf format and one can comprehensively print the required content of references.

(c) **Search Filters**: The Advanced Search feature is extremely fast and flexible and helps in locating parameter specific records. This search provides two filter options for conducting in incisive search.

(a) Search text on the basis of: Keywords; article title; author, journal volume, journal issue; Initial pages and year.

(b) Search text in: All journals or individual /specific database.

Other e-repositories

The Institutional Repositories (IRs) other then e-journals are created using Dspace. There are several communities and collections in these IRs. (i) articles database (ii) photo-gallery (iii) pre-prints (iv) presentations (v) Seminar Reports. Besides these repositories there are other collections that are offered as digital repositories (i) the fellowship records, a unique collection of the INSA archives. Development of repositories for new collections/ communities are in pipeline.

Usage

While the e-publishing of Academy journals project was being envisaged, there were apprehensions pertaining to (i) usage patterns to justify the creation and sustenance of the repository taking into account the resource intensiveness of the project; (ii) fear of fall in existing number of print subscriptions. This is a global phenomenon at least when INSA created it that time, a time frame of one to one an half years was required to let users settle down with the new form which was partially due to visibility factor of the repository. Today the web log to our repositories given multifaceted information inputs. It may also be worthwhile to mention here that the availability of online version has not affected the number of subscriptions to the print versions of the journals, which are priced publications.

Epilogue

e-publishing is definitely a new paradigm for scholarly publishing. It is not only about technology, it's about change in social practices Technological changes in publishing and in access to information are leading to changes in relationships and business models.

e-publishing will breed and succeed applying best practices. Critical success factors like understanding the information ecology; managing business old & new streams; preserve existing readership while building the new; Cost control, partnership building, and the like needs to be well thought of. While simple site designs and navigational features, clarity on copyright policy, long term archiving, lobbying for funding support for online publishing, practicing open access to maximize impact and relying on open standards document formats and open source software servers would be definite advantageous.

Publisher's and Titles

One of the constant irritations of both the librarian and publishers life is the transferal of titles between publishers. There is the uncertainty before the librarians what will happen to their current electronic access, URL links, perpetual access rights, the price or impose a charge for them.

Some work has been done to create standards for these movements and changes: The STM committee has recently also drafted guidelines which were discussed during their February meeting. This document attempts to ensure that a customers' experience is not altered during a title move, and from the journals perspective, to ensure that readership is not lost.

The ALPSP (Association of Learned Society Publishers) attempted to create a best practice document such as:

(a) Contracts must establish "Who owns what".

(b) Customer licenses must be clear on what will happen in the event of a change

(c) Content should continue to be available for customers

(d) Both publishers to continue to offer parallel access for at least 6 months or made free.

(e) Archive should be created via a trusted third party, e.g. a deposit library.

(f) Access to prior subscribers should be maintained, either by: free access, CD-ROM or local load, by passing IP details to the new publisher.

(g) Transferring publisher to bear the cost if perpetual rights were offered to the customer.

(h) Journal URL to be passed to new publisher

(i) Subscription info and payments to be passed to receiving publisher

(j) Ownership of subscriber and member list to be clarified in contract.

(k) Extension of grace periods

The rapid development in the area of publishing is more in the area of electronic publishing, where Internet has changed the publishing scenario from traditional to electronic. Now resources are known as e-document, e-resources, e-books, e-journals etc. This change has been influencing the publishers, suppliers, and subscription agents for offering additional access facility of journals in electronic format. An electronic journal provides extra services of 24x7 hour uninterrupted access through Internet to the users at their desktop. Further, a gateway portal of electronic journals acting as vital guide and quick catalogue service to the users for retrieving and browsing their desired information from the thousands of interdisciplinary journals.

American and European publishers publish their scholarly journals in electronic format with additional supports of archiving, storing, managing, indexing, abstracting, searching, accessing, and cross-linking of bibliographic references within the articles for easy access and wider coverage. Recently J-Gate has also launched its an Open J-Gate portal for free access of 3723 electronic journals published by various organizations globally on open access platform. There are some other initiatives of electronic publishing created landmark in the industry such as OpenMed on medical, Medknow Publications on medical, and IndianJournals.com etc. based on mostly open access available merely in English language. Some of the journals are on free access on web and few of them are on subscription basis. At the same time, wider indexing and peer review process are main concern for these journals, which are mostly not introduced on greater strengths, as it should be.

INFLIBNET Initiative

INFLIBNET is a National Centre established by UGC (University Grants Commission) under MHRD (Ministry of Human Resource Development), Government of India, for promoting library automation, resource sharing, cooperative development among the academic libraries and other R&D libraries in India. The Centre is directed towards modernization of libraries and information centers and aims at establishing a mechanism for information transfer and access to scholarship, learning and academic pursuits. It has constituted a national network of universities and consortium called "UGC-Infonet" and E-Journal Consortium", respectively. Some other initiatives taken by INFLIBNET are.

(a) providing funds for ICT infrastructure and environment to the universities.

(b) developing various union databases of the library resources such as books, theses/dissertations and serials including the profiles of the subject experts working in universities and R&D Institutes.

(c) conducting various training programs for library practitioners time to time.

(d) making available multilingual integrated user friendly library house keeping software SOUL based on Unicode supporting MARC bibliographic standards on minimum cost to the academic[21] community of the country.

(e) working as an information pool for the users of the country by having created six document delivery centers region and subject-wise.

Electronic publishing has become more and more popular especially in the academic community.

According to Gordon Wills electronic publishing is "The exploitation of electronics in any and every cost-effective and cost-beneficial way that can facilitate the processes of publishing, where publishing for our purpose means: Conceiving, creating, capturing, transforming, disseminating, archiving, searching, and retrieving academic and professional knowledge and information".

Electronic publishing process consists of four steps:

(a) Creation;

(b) Text;

(c) Publishing; and

(d) Maintenance

Electronic publishing is new dimension in the area of printing/ publication, which is redefined with evolution of technology. Electronic publishing is still in infancy form and needs lot of advancements and changes. Various gateway portals help at some extents that google scholar helps in finding out the articles, Google Print helps in finding out the books including the additional information about a book and its subject. Promotional print catalogue and CD-ROM are the tools for the publishers in bridging the gaps between the users and their desired publications. There are many positive reasons behind choosing electronic publishing of scholarly journals:

(a) Process of the print publishing is same as the electronic publishing

(b) Universities and research institutions in India have lots of scientific publications publishing in different Indian languages on various subjects, needs visibility.

(c) Electronic version of journals gets wider exposure to research scholars.

(d) Availability in electronic format of the intellectual contents changes learning behavior of the user.

(e) The Universities have lagged behind due to lack of fund, support and skill in this area and need training to make their journals online.

(f) It has brought down the over all time log of publishing from article submission to its final publications.

12
e-Journal

The academic journal, far from being timeless or inevitable, is a highly-contingent academic structure. It came into being in the seventeenth century as scholars in various fields shifted their standard medium of communication from writing to print. In the Middle Ages and the Renaissance, scholars publicized their ideas and discoveries by writing letters to each other. In the 1660s, the first scholarly journals collected the latest letters and printed them for the convenience of a "mass" academic audience; ultimately, the journals evolved into collections of articles which retained little of their initial epistolary nature. Secondly, new technologies which are initially conceived or applied as imitations or extensions of old formats soon tend to find their own identities and their own formats. In the transportation industry, for example, the first automobiles were treated as relatively innocuous – or ridiculous – "horseless carriages". In communications, early television was considered and largely used as an electronic purveyor of stage plays. In academia, before the days of journals, print was seen as a medium for replicating individual scholarly letters. The current move towards electronic journals can be analyzed in the same terms: almost instinctively, our first application of Internet technology to scholarly communication has been to create an electronic equivalent of the journals.

Third by, certain academic disciplines having a reputation for technological sophistication are rapidly moving away from the journal model. The best example of such a discipline is physics, which, since 1991, has had the benefit of a massive "archive" of electronically self-published pre-prints developed by Paul Ginsparg at Los Alamos National Laboratory in New Mexico. History is repeated: in the seventeenth century, physicists and other scientists, rather than traditional literary, historical and legal scholars – were the first to had for the technological "promised land" of the print-based journal.

Advantages of e-Journals

1. Higher rate of acceptance of articles.
2. Increased speed in the peer review and publication process.
3. Possible acceptance by editors of more articles.
4. Lower production and delivery costs.
6. Use of different models for format during publication.
7. Use of sophisticated searching strategies and software.
8. Distribution and correspondence not limited by time and geography.

Problems with e-Journals

1. e-journals do not carry the same weight as print journals in academic credit and advancement decisions;
2. e-journals are neither accepted nor supported by universities because e-journals publishing efforts may not be recognized as an official university activity.
3. The peer interest that generates the authorship and readership of print journals may not exist.
4. Necessary access to the computer and telecommunication system cannot be taken for granted.
5. Users may not be trained in the use of Internet.

Electronic Journals of Academic and Special Librarianship

Librarian are both a creation and a servant of society. A library operates routinely with a known set of customers. A library also operates on trust. When a client walks into the library, he trusts that he will get the material or information that he needs. The library, in turn, trusts that the client will return the items within the specified borrowing period. The specific structure of a library with its strict requirements as to efficiency demands a focus on the quality of value-adding processes. If a library is to be managed according to quality criteria, quality needs to be defined and made measurable. The indicators found must be captured in a measuring system for the sectors "cost and performance", "customer satisfaction", and "staff satisfaction" that facilitates quality controlling and provides staff with controlling parameters for everyday work.

The history of marketing library services began long before the concept was born. Sameul Swett Green in his often quoted speech at the ALA Conference in 1876 advocated "improved personal relations between librarians and readers".

Basic Steps

Librarians and information professionals must learn to effectively market and their services:

1. ***Customers*** – Libraries are part of a highly competitive service industry. Competition comes from mega-bookstores, online book dealers, consultants, the Internet, and individuals who feel they can go it alone. Free web access to information is here to stay and non-library and fee access information providers won't hesitate to market to library customers.
2. ***Resources*** – Libraries of all types have to compete with other organizations or departments for funds. Special libraries find their funding is frequently targeted during parent organization budget cuts. Marketing library services benefits the bottom line.
3. ***Relevance*** – Libraries need to market themselves to remain connected with their communities and have some bearing on real-world issues and present-day events.
4. ***Stop being taken for granted*** – Libraries need to convey what is unique about the access and services they provide.

5. ***Promote an updated image*** – Librarians are not perceived as well-trained, technologically savvy information experts. Most customers do not see the demanding information management responsibilities of a librarian.
6. ***Visibility*** – Librarians are not on the radar screens of many people who think of themselves as information literate.
7. ***Community resource*** – Libraries are and should be viewed as essential and valuable community resources. People need to be made aware of the services and products that are provided and their comparative value. Librarians should be the resources.
8. ***Rising expectations*** – Library users expect recognition, attention, and appreciation for their individual information needs. Customers also have ever-changing needs and wants, which makes the library market as dynamic as retail markets.

Survival

Libraries depend on the support of others for their existence. A library must communicate and work with its customers and governing/funding entities to provide information about what the library is doing and to enable the library to learn about the community it serves.

Library image

Effective marketing can among other things: increase library funds, increase usage of services, educate customers and non-customers, change perceptions, and enhance the clout and reputation of the library and its staff.

Most librarians do market libraries on the following steps:

1. Students should use library databases to locate quality information for their papers.
2. Faculty should send their students to librarians for assistance.
3. Children should be brought to the library to learn about books.

4. Middle managers should tap into the corporate library for information.
5. Librarians may be reluctant to capitalize on their strengths and knowledge, while the general public often does not see the value that information professionals could bring to sophisticated information challenges.
6. There is a belief that libraries do not need to be promoted in any special way because their importance to society should be apparent to all.
7. Librarians and libraries are limited by their traditional image; that libraries offer books for lending and provide programming for children.
8. Marketing is more widely discussed and accepted professionally than in the past, this acceptance hasn't necessarily resulted in more marketing classes in library schools' curricula.
9. Marketing is a business tool and not applicable to library settings.
10. Librarians have a fear of commercial publicity and see marketing as manipulative, a waste of time and resources, and unprofessional.
11. Librarians often wait for customers to come to them, librarians push customers to stand by the facility or use across the library web site.
12. Marketing is a complicated problem for libraries because of their wide range of products and services from books to Internet access, and an extremely diverse audience that ranges from children to seniors, public officials to business people, and students to faculty, etc.
13. Lack of funds is often used as a reason or excuse not to market. Marketing is also a matter of improving the customer's experience of library services.

Total Quality Management

Total quality management is an approach that an organization takes for improving its performance on systematic and continuous basis. This achieved by involving all employees throughout the organization in satisfying all requirements of every customer, either external or internal. Quality Management is the basis for library management in general.

There are some principles of TQM as meeting the customers needs, exact assessment, continuous improvement, teamwork, and enthusiasm of the leaders are typical for library service.

1. ***Total*** – Everyone in the organization is involved in creating and maintaining the quality of the services and products offered.
2. ***Quality*** – The organization through individual and collective actions focuses on meeting customer needs, recognizing that customer perception identifies quality.
3. ***Management*** – In managing the system, the emphasis lies on continuously improving the system in order to achieve the best results.

TQM is a management philosophy embracing all activities through which the needs of the customer and the community, and the objectives of the organization, are satisfied in the most efficient and cost effective way by maximizing the potential of all employees in a continuing drive for improvement.

Basic Tools of TQM

Management tools that can be used for measuring and documenting quality of the products, processes and services are as follows:

(a) Control charts
(b) Pareto chart
(c) Cause and effect diagram
(d) Run charts
(e) Histogram
(f) Scattered diagram
(g) Flow charts

It is giving personal service and efficient back room preparation. It is managing this moment's transaction and the whole experience for the customer. It is providing value and maintaining a distinction. To achieve all of this dynamically, the quality leader needs data and mech. nisms to provide it. He needs a minimum of four channels of information:

1. to keep him in touch with the customer's changing requirements;
2. to monitor his output against those requirements;
3. to feedback his performance in matching the two; and
4. to anticipate his customers needs and help keep him one step ahead.

TQM : Importance

Libraries are among the most ancient social and cultural institutions in existence. Ancient libraries as well as modern ones have one thing in common: all of them have a body of information recorded on some type of medium and that information could be retrieved when needed. The accessibility of information requires good organizational ability from those who are in charge. The basic concern is to create a structure of the organization where desired information is retrieved and made accessible efficiently and in a timely manner to the users. Creation and maintenance of such a structure requires an effective management process that facilitates work toward that goal.

A library is a business that must be operated efficiently and well. A major difference is that most libraries are non-profit organizations. Management of vast amounts of information stored in different formats – printed, electronic, audio, video – requires use of the most modern management techniques.

Today technologies have changed our social and economic life. In the workplace methodologies change; people work at home or on the web with flexible timetables, and more and more virtual communities are emerging in different fields. The most important stakeholders in the library are customers. These are interested, for various reasons, in the introduction of TQM. The introduction of TQM makes great demands on the staff.

Factors

1. TQM involves a process of change and therefore requires of staff that they be ready to play a constructive role in that process.
2. TQM requires a basic reorientation from the media stock towards customers and markets. For TQM a result-oriented approach, not the input of resources, is of vital importance.
3. Rewarding for both staff and the institution: improve- ment of the institution in which they work, a strengthening of that institution's position, and more opportunity of staff to influence their own work.

The management of quality in libraries, as a management method that allows the improvement of performance, has been the object of interest for the managers of these services.

The technology is already superb and has even greater potential, but needs the wisdom of older minds that are trained and have built a lifetime of experience in making sure people get the information they need. Librarians are quickly responding to the challenge and are making sure they get their share of the information age financial largesse. Marketing in libraries has gone beyond special days and book displays. The value of marketing library's products and services has been recognized and need to develop and formalize our marketing strategies. Sell the idea to your manager and other staff by aligning your strategies to your organisation's strategic function and business plan.

13

e-Writing

The ability to communicate orally, using symbols to convey both concrete and abstract information, distinguishes the human race. Yet, before the development of a means to record language, communication was limited by individual capacities for memory and cognition. Oral discourse relies on sound, which is evanescent, having meaning only when it is going out of existence. This evanescence of sound is what gives rise to the cognitive and expressive characteristics that distinguish 'orality'. Oral language is limited by the memory of the individual, leading to an emphasis on formulas and mnemonic structures. For the same reason, oral language is additive rather than subordinative, aggregative rather than analytic, redundant, and conservative. It is close to the 'human life world'.

Although symbolic language enabled a significant number of human achievements. It was not until humans developed a means to record language that human society could really expand and grow. Writing enabled societies not only to expand but also to communicate across the boundaries of space and time. Of equal importance are the cognitive and expressive consequences of chirography (handwriting). Although writing builds on the symbolic an rule-based systems of oral language, it requires knowledge of an alphabetic (or pictographic) symbol system, and of chirography. With the developments of literate skills come cognitive and expressive (language-use) changes such as detachment. Writing encourages abstract and analytic thought: The durability of written language removes the necessity for mnemonic characteristics of oral language; people can refer back to written text and are not constrained to organize it in ways that encourage memory (such as setting content to songs or chants). The lack of presence of the other is compensated for by textual cues like punctuation and by recognized conventions of grammar and usage that help the reader understand who is being spoken about, for instance.

Written expression is dependent entirely on the alphabetic word — and not on the visual and vocal elements that help people communicate in face-to-face speech. Writing requires a codifiable medium to convey meaning. Also, it uses a vocabulary, based on known conventions and rules of usages, to create new ideas. In written expression, discrete elements (the alphabet) are combined and recombined to help convey new ideas, often using new words created to meet the needs of conveying those new ideas. Finally, written language must have a fixed relationship with spoken language, so that people can communicate the same thought in two different media simultaneously — as in reading to one another. These elements give writing its characteristics of permanence and completeness. Written language is less redundant, more planned. Meaning and shades of meaning are conveyed by carefully chosen and placed words. Meaning may be modified by deleting, editing, and otherwise changing the written words, unlike oral language, where once words are said out loud, they cannot be unsaid, only explained. In written language, the presence of the receiver is not required, and the constraints of time and space are removed. Hence writing can be more analytical than oral communication.

With the mechanization of writing, the characteristics of written language were refined and expanded:

(1) The invention of print led to the expansion of literacy.

(2) Print concretized the permanence of writing. Until the printing press, writing was fragile, with its permanence dependent on the preservation of an often single piece of parchment or reed.

(3) Print introduced durability and multiple copies, and "embedded the word in (visual) space more definitively".

It also introduced hierarchies, which in turn introduced lists and indexes.

(4) It reinforced the linearity and sequentiality of writing.

(5) The permanent nature of print also led to the preservation of language. The Mass dissemination of printed texts meant both fixity and standardization of content.

(6) Print arrested linguistic drift, standardized language, and eventually led to the deliberate codification of written language.

(7) The proliferation of printed texts also led to the establishment of research and the development of the scientific method.

(8) The analytic element introduced by writing was reinforced by print, with a corresponding focus on logic. Increased availability and affordability of printed texts enabled the development of the modern educational system.

(9) The development of the modern sense of personal privacy and private ownership.

(10) As books became portable and affordable, reading became a solitary rather than a social activity.

(11) The printing press laid the foundation for today's models of commercial writing, introducing the concepts of ownership and mass publication.

The Impact of Computers on Traditional Writing

The computer, developed in the mid-twentieth century, is undeniably a product of a literate and technological society. Electronic writing is a singular product of the computer age and the electronic writing enabled by computers has affected traditional writing significantly.

Electronic writing refers to the conglomerate of writing that can be done on and through the medium of a networked computer. This includes writing for asynchronous interpersonal communication (as in e-mail, mailing lists, newsgroups, and discussion groups).

Computers re-introduce many oral characteristics into electronic writing. Computers are unique in that they introduce characteristics that go beyond the secondary orality evident in television, film, and other electronic media. For instance, although computers rely on an alphabetical or symbolic lexicon, they are more than a print-reliant or "literate" medium. Computers rely on an alphabetical or symbolic lexicon, they are more than a print-reliant or "literate" medium. Computers utilize print in a flexible manner, allowing immediacy in communication, while enabling a concentration on the present moment, and eliminating distance between users — all oral characteristics.

Computer communication allows the reader to manipulate content, and less "literate" than the print from which it stems. The reader can interact with the text on an immediate, physical level; roles of writers and readers thus become unclear. The experience becomes fragmentary and malleable, or oral, rather than unified and stable, or literate and information retains a fluidity in computer-mediated communication that it lacks in traditional literacy. Electronic writing is characterized by the use of oral conventions over traditional conventions, of argument over exposition, and of group thinking over individual thinking. Computer users often treat electronic writing as an oral medium: communication is often fragmented, computer-mediated communication is used for phatic communion, and formulaic devices have arisen. Like primary orality, electronic communication is often "language of action". Electronic writing thus transforms traditional writing by introducing oral elements that differentiate it from secondary orality. Computers incorporate a new orality by bringing new perspectives to the manipulation and understanding of writing. The text becomes more immediate, more fragmented and fluid, and the medium offers greater capacity for individual participation and interactivity.

Computers also remain technologically based and grounded in the abstract, analytical, literate modes of thought that govern traditional writing. Many scholars consider computers to be a text-based medium reliant on the conventions of literacy. Ideas are expressed in a logical, linear fashion, and linear narrative forms govern most traditional writing. Electronic writing, however, subverts traditional conventions of linearity, both in interpersonal communication online and in the use of hypertext on the Web. Hypertext, the language of the Web, is a non-linear language that is dynamic and non-sequential and connects information through nodes or links. Hypertext frequently incorporates multimedia, principally graphics and sound. Nevertheless, hypertext dramatically changes traditional writing, not only removing the linear imperative, but by substantially impacting common literary and grammatical conventions. Due to its emphasis on connectivity rather than linearity, hypertext discourages the use of coherent narrative. Traditional writing delivers a coherent narrative in large chunks of text; large chunks of text defeat the purpose of hypertext. Hypertext allows writers to organize information loosely, rather than in a well-developed thesis.

Fixity to Fluidity

Traditional writing and print is the fixity of the word on the page. Electronic writing, especially hypertext, lacks this fixity, existing as it does in cyberspace. Electronic text is always fluid; it is never fixed. It remains ever dynamic and subject to change and modification. Writing posted to the Web in hypertext is never finished, as it can not only be updated and revised at will, but its nature can be changed as other writers link to it. Electronic text is thus not only a fluid network of writing, but it is also a fluid network of information and interpersonal.

Relatedly, (1) With electronic writing, the permanence of the written artifact no longer exists, taking away from electronic writing an integral feature of print. (2) Written and printed texts provide readers with a concrete artifact that encourages backward and forward scanning. (3) Electronic writing, whether it be an e-mail or a Web document, exists only in electronic space, providing the reader with vanishing words on a screen rather than a written artifact with concrete presence. (4) It is this lack of permanence that leads many computer users to record data on disks or on paper.

As the medium for electronic writing, binary computer language with its 0s and 1s is a significant factor in altering the fixity of the written word on the printed page. Alphabetic writing is rigid in that it relies on a finite alphabet, combined in words that are expressed on the written page in a specific linear order and sequence. Binary code can be used to represent any character set, and therefore is not tied to a specific language or culture. The complexity of visual and graphic forms in hypertext calls for non-discursive reading and writing. Therefore electronic writing opposes the standardization of language encouraged by the traditional text.

Interactivity also distinguishes electronic writing from traditional writing. The Web is a global hypertext system unique in its capacity to interface with other systems. The use of embedded links allows interactivity between the reader, author, and medium. This not only creates a unique convergence of mass media and interpersonal media where the consumer can become the provider of information, but it allows a unique re-negotiation of the writer-audience relationship. A reader perusing a traditional text is bound by the linear, two-dimensional nature of the printed word on the page to follow where the author leads. Reading traditional texts is a passive and solitary activity; reading electronic texts is an active and engaging process, as the reader makes choices about where to go, and then navigates using links and online forms to get there.

The organization of the material must be visually appealing and must take advantage of the unique interactive features of the Web. In traditional writing the publisher or editor makes material available and visually appealing; in cyber-writing. The cyber-writer often also must be editor and designer, considering issues of file structure, graphic design, and navigability. Writing becomes even more complex because the writer has little control over the paths readers will take through the hyperlinks.

Writer's need to learn new and changing technologies is a significant feature. Although most computer word-processing has the capability of conversion to hypertext, electronic writing requires a knowledge of computers and software. Skilled electronic writers need to incorporate the latest information-organization and design technologies.

A singular feature of electronic writing is that it allows anyone with access to a networked computer to "publish" on the Internet. Today's sophisticated and user-friendly software makes it easy for entry-level writers to publish their writing on the Web. Through global search engines and linking, cyber-writers have the potential to reach a large reading public, and writing to a sizable audience thus becomes an option not open to most writers in non-electronic print. Each specialized genre of traditional writing has its own standards for quality of content. Value is a measure of how strongly something is desired..... expressed in terms of the effort one is willing to spend in acquiring it. Given that all navigation in cyberspace requires time, interest, and access to technology, any writing that leads the reader to seek it out can be called good writing. Computers are still a developing technology, drawing any definitive conclusions about the effect of electronic writing on traditional standards of quality may be premature. It is important to note, however, that while cyberspace is still a medium defining itself, it is one where writers are in the unique position of shaping the development of standards and norms of writing — a time that is long past in traditional writing.

Computers are currently seen as electronic extensions of prevailing models of literacy, and electronic writing is generally compared to print. It is easy to understand why scholars have come to this conclusion: although electronic writing requires that authors learn new technologies, incorporate new interactive techniques, and gain expertise in design-related issues of presentation, the conventions and traditions of print are still the touchstone. While electronic writing may require that authors learn new technologies, acknowledge the need for incorporation of new interactive techniques, and gain expertise in design-related issues of presentation, at its heart the print metaphor sees electronic writing as following the conventions and traditions of print. Computers are still in development and the possibility of a concept change exists. Whichever model comes to be accepted will influence the practice and understanding of electronic writing. Going from a print to an oral metaphor will emphasize the importance of interactivity rather than the forms of traditional writing.

14
e-Literature

"Information is the oxygen of the modern age. It seeps through the walls topped by barbed wire, it wafts across the electrified borders".

Ronald Reagan

Electronic books (e-books) are becoming a valuable addition to the print collections of libraries. Libraries are now taking part in trials of those e-book databases that can support their client's information needs.

Extraterritorial application of electronic literature is an important aspect dealing with extraterritoriality.

S.R. Ranganathan in his Five Laws of Library Science states, "Books are for Use". Though this law was pronounced in 1930's, it leads to wider application in the context of the Internet. The Internet has changed this law into "Books are for All" for global applications. The use of books by all could be by paying a nominal amount through electronic sources or getting free access to the literature. A Google search was made on free e-books that listed nearly 20 million sites that lead to a large number of titles by great authors of the past.

Free-eBooks.net specializes in collecting free fiction, tutorial, marketing and business eBooks. The site has links to resources for eBook Publishers. It has preferred categories of free e-books on Art, Fashion, comics, health, literature, philosophy, psychology etc.

Project Gutenberg

Project Gutenberg is the Internet's oldest producer of FREE electronic books (e-Books or e-Texts) on the Internet. The collection has more than 19.000 e-Books produced by hundreds of volunteers. The Project Gutenberg Philosophy is to make information, books and other materials available to the general public in forms a vast majority of the computers, programs and people can easily read, use, quote, and search. In October 2003, Project Gutenberg added the 10,000th e-Books to its collection. In the first 11 weeks of 2004, Project Gutenberg added 313 new e-Books.

Mission

The mission of Project Gutenberg is "To encourage the creation and distribution of e-Books. This mission is, as much as possible, to encourage all those who are interested in making e-Books and helping to give them away. Project Gutenberg has given the freedom to volunteers in the choices of which books to distribute, which formats to convert them, or any other ideas they may have concerning "the creation and distribution of e-Books". There are no membership requirements and therefore there are no limits to the amount of people that can get involved.

Literature and Culture are key factors essential for the continuation of any society. IT professionals and people who work for this Project are volunteers. The main purpose for running such a project is to make literature widely spread to as many generations as well as helping people to acquire skills for locating the e-texts or other electronic materials they need. They are also available in different languages. People from different background and cultures can preserve and carry on they culture they belong to for their next generations. Copyright varies in different countries and some people may take advantage of this fact to make profit for them. For example, one can obtain an e-book for free from another country but it may be still copyrighted in his/her own country. It is possible to distribute and sell the books for profit.

Consideration to Every Individual

Project Gutenberg uses the simplest format of text that not only gives consideration to general public, but also those with disabilities such as blind or visually impaired. Indeed the plain text has provided the ease of accessing literature in many ways. "Once text is in the PC, it can be enlarged by a word processor, read by a text-to-speech program, or punched out by a Braille printer". A personal computer holds the key to helping people with disabilities. Project Gutenberg has a number of classic books free to download, given the copyright issues are satisfied.

15

e-Learning in Distance Education

These are print, audio/video broadcasting, audio/video teleconferencing, computer aided instruction, e-learning/ online-learning, computer broadcasting/podcasting etc. Yet the radio remains a very viable form, especially in the developing nations, because of its reach. In India the FM Channel is very popular and is being used by the national open university (the Indira Gandhi National Open University) and its consortia plus the state open universities, to broadcast educational programmes of variety on areas such as teacher education, rural development, programmes in agriculture for farmers, science education, creative writing, mass communication, in addition to traditional courses in liberal arts, science and business administration.

Distance education as the basic approach in the Open University systems has acquired considerable significance in promoting both education and professional well being of the community through new communication technologies open. Education acquires a definite role in developing the right kind of social values, attitudes and habits among the weaker sections, disadvantaged including tribal as they contribute a big share to achieve an acceptable overall national growth.

Significant of Distant Education

The disadvantaged groups suffer from a high degree of variety. This variability can be seen through their sex, culture, caste, social status, economic condition geographical location.

The conventional system of education will never be able uplift their living style and change their conservative mindset. Owing to its distinctive features like flexibility, multimedia approach, learning support and individualized study, this system is best suited for mass education. The inability of the conventional system of education in reaching the larger segment of the Indian population and democratizing education perhaps compelled the national leaders to think of an alternative viable medium of disseminating education. Evolution of open and distance learning system in India was the result of this compression.

Distance Education

(a) Correspondence connected through regular mail

(b) Internet conducted either synchronously or asynchronously

(c) Tele-course/Broadcast where content is delivered via radio or television.

(d) CD-ROM where the students interact with computer content stored on a CD-ROM

E-learning needs to be linked with the process of learning as the it is not only capable of overcoming the barriers that distance presents but also changed the very nature of the instructional process. It is technology that made the move from correspondence to distance education possible.

Yet the efforts to integrate E-learning are not at all sufficient viewing the vast panorama of illiterate disadvantaged Indians many more drastic steps directed to the all round educational development of the disadvantaged are required to be taken.

In Distant Education Choice of media is crucial as there is no provision for face to face interaction and the students depend on print material with occasional face to face support. Education was imparted with the help of maps, charts, pictures, books, diagrams, and till recently through 11mm projectors for educational purposes. The present day mechanical devices have brought about a virtual revolution in diverse field of human activity.

Electronic Medias used in Distant Education

Distance education uses different media: books, mail, radio, gramophone records and audiocassettes, film, television, cable and satellite television, video, multimedia systems, CD-ROM media, e-mail, Internet/web. It also uses two-way media for communication between the instructor and students such as radio, telephone, voice mail, instant messaging, chat, mailing lists and web forums. Each of the mentioned media has specific advantages and shortcomings.

Radio is an effective medium and has been extensively used for educational purposes to spread literacy or to give formal or non-formal education all over the world. Lessons are planned and written for broadcast from All India Radio and IGNOU Radio programmes supplement radio is with in the reach of common man and can be carried along from place to place.

Television is more powerful and expressive. T.V. lessons are entertaining as well as attractive. The television screen may become the electronic blackboard of the future.

Computer applications for distance education fall into four broad categories:

***Computer Assisted Instruction* (*CAI*)** – uses the computer as a self-contained teaching machine to present discrete lessons to achieve specific but limited educational objectives. There are several CAI modes, including: drill and practice, tutorial, simulations and games, and problem-solving.

***Computer Managed Instruction* (*CMI*)** – uses the computer's branching, storage, and retrieval capabilities to organize instruction and track student records and progress. The instruction need not be delivered via computer, although often CAI (the instructional component) is combined with CMI.

***Computer Mediated Communication* (*CMC*)** – describes computer applications that facilitate communication. Examples include electronic mail, computer conferencing, and electronic bulletin boards.

Computer-Based Multimedia – HyperCard, hyper-media, and a still-developing generation of powerful, sophisticated, and flexible computing tools have gained the attention of distance educators in recent years. The goal of computer-based multimedia is to integrate various voice, video, and computer technologies into a single, easily accessible delivery system.

The Internet and Distance Education

The Internet is the largest, most powerful computer network in the world. As more and more colleges, universities, schools, companies, and private citizens connect to the Internet either through affiliations with regional not-for-profit networks or by subscribing to information services provided by for-profit companies, more possibilities are opened for distance educators to overcome time and distance to reach students.

Like postal mail, e-mail is used to exchange messages or other information with people. Instead of being delivered by the postal service to a postal address, e-mail is delivered by Internet software through a computer network to a computer address. Many bulletin boards can be accessed through the Internet. Two common public bulletin boards on the Internet are USENET and LISTSERV. USENET is a collection of thousands of topically organized newsgroups,

WWW:

The WWW is an exciting and innovative front-end to the Internet. Officially WWW is described as a "....wide-area hypermedia information retrieval initiative aiming to give universal access to a large universe of documents".

Satellite

Satellite is the other glamorous medium in Distance Education. It is used for communicating over long distance. More channels for both radio and television are possible because of the satellite programmes viewed by people in cities as well as in countryside locations. The communication channels are not affected by natural calamities as is usually the case with telephone wires.

Video Conferencing

Video conferencing is a video communication session among three or more people, who are geographically separated. In video conferencing technology, two or more people at different locations can see and hear each other at the same time, sometimes even share computer applications for collaboration. Video conferencing offers possibilities for school, colleges and libraries to use these systems for a variety of purposes. A video conferencing system requires the audiovisual equipment, which includes a monitor, camera, microphone, and speaker and a means of transmission. Rather than an internet based connection, such as that used by webcams, which have to share bandwidth with other Internet data, a compressed video system on a dedicated band with provides smooth audio and video should be incorporated.

(a) It eliminates expensive travel

(b) It makes the best use of limited time

(c) It allows genuine dialogue between all participants.

(d) It allows immediate, full two way communication of content – verbal, pictorial objects etc.

(e) It provides a sense of social presence.

It is an intimate method of communication on an individual or small group basis. It does not replace the use of print or other methods used in the conceptualization process. Its can be used to encourage construction, its true use lies in encouraging dialogue and increasing the scope for dialogue.

Convenience

(a) Courses are accessible on the schedule.

(b) E-Learning does not require physical attendance.

(c) Learning is self-paced (not too slow, not too fast).

(d) Students are unbound by time – courses are available 24/7.

(e) Students are unbound by place – study at home, work, or on the road.

(f) Read materials online or download them for reading later.

Flexibility

(a) E-Learning accommodates the preferences and needs – it's student-centered.

(b) Choose instructor-led or self-study courses.

(c) Skip over material you already know and focus on topics you'd like to learn.

(d) Use the tools best suited to your learning styles.

Limitations of E-Learning

Widespread computer illiteracy still exists. It has been observed students do not feel as comfortable in online collaborative learning environments as in classroom settings, especially adult learners. Moreover some novice computer users may experience difficulties of anxiety when using a new online application other students may feel confused and become lost or overloaded by disorganized purposeless or opinionated dialogues that come across over the online discussion.

Real Time Services

A new and exciting method of digital reference service that libraries are attempting to provide more and more now is live reference. These are real-time, interactive reference services in which the users can talk to a real, live reference librarian at any time, from anywhere in the world. The librarian can perform Internet searches and push websites onto the user's browser, and can receive immediate feedback from the users. Most libraries currently involved in real time reference service are part of collaborative network so that they can share staffing and work around the clock to truly provide reference service any time.

Steps

(a) On-line tutor training courses to be taken up, the prime objective of the online tutors would be to create pool of tutors.

(b) Creation and Development of communication infra-structure to permit experimental delivery of the early on-line training courses involved.

(c) Accurately manage and measure each stage of the program's execution.

(d) Convenient program distribution to multiple locations.

(e) The web based training management system must allow customized curricula, as well as changes and updates to a data base from one central location.

(f) Students must be highly motivated and proficient in computer operation before they can successfully function in a computer-based distance learning environment.

(g) High flexibility must be given to the orchestration of learning material by giving freedom to manipulate, modify and customize it to one's needs.

(h) Multimedia technologies steaming audio and video animations.

(i) Internet and WWW access to ensure equal opportunities for computer interaction and feedback.

(j) e-mail can help the instructor provide feedback more quickly than surface mail or telephone. Prompt response generally increases student motivation and performance.

16

e-Resources

Library is a product of a society which gives satisfaction to every sector of social structure. Library is a learning centre to the mass and represent as one unit of a democratic world. It is the primary objective of the educational policy to eradicate the illiteracy. It intended to serve the educational need of all sex and level of human being from child, adult and elderly people. It supplement the work of the schools and developing the reading tastes of children and young people. The main objectives of a library are:

(a) to establish the educational and social norms
(b) to provide services to the users
(c) to open the doors for free access to all members of the community

According to Dr. C.K. Sharma, a library serve the community:

(a) Children, adults, elderly persons and all other persons live in a society through public libraries.
(b) Students, faculty and research scholars through Academic libraries.
(c) Scientists, doctors, engineers, technologists and other professionals through special libraries.
(d) Industrialists, businessmen, managers, market persons and others related business, trade and industry through technical or business libraries.

In fact all the three types of libraries are said to be open-access libraries. Any user may consult the library at anytime without any different of cast, colour and creed or any cader and status. The main purpose of the open access is to:

(a) give entertainment,

(b) provide educational service,

(c) provide cultural knowledge and information,

(d) provide informational service

Advent of information and communication technology have revolutionized the human activity. University libraries, public libraries and special libraries exploit optimum available infrastructure on the campus including various e-resources.

There are three types of resources:

1. Primary – original products
2. Secondary – Products based on original products
3. Tertiary – Products used for reference and directions

There are two kinds of resources:

1. Book and non-book material – Books, periodicals, reports, conference proceedings, patents, standards, and other source of informations.
2. Electronic Resources – CD, Cassettes, CD-ROM, through internet, Networks, e-mail, fax from Database, information centers, etc.

Now web based electronic resources have become most popular tools for academic research. It is because e-resources are an upto date source of information and they can be accessed from any computer which can be connected with any network and the internet.

Some of the e-Resources are:

1. Full text online database
2. Search engine
3. Eric

Open Sources

1. ***INDEST Consortium***: Ministry of Human Resources Development, Government of India established Indian

Digital Library in Engineering Science and Technology (INDEST) consortium and provided necessary funds for its applicability in providing different access to electronic resources subscribed for the consortium to the core members like Indian Institutes of Technology Libraries, Science and Technology libraries for their resource sharing projects. Its services have been extended to member institutes and educational institutions. Under this project on-line access is provided to IEEE/IEE Electronic libraries (IEL), ASCE and ASME to our universities.

2. ***UGC – Infonet Consortium***: It is e-journal consortium. UGC has initiated the UGC-Infonet under the consortium project in India. About 5000 scholarly journals are electronically provided with full text to the academic and research libraries. These e-journals are generally related to science and technology. 25 publishers have been included in this consortium from the global network. These e-journals can be accessed globally by the technical and research institutes on a nominal charges. This consortium provides current as well as archival to core and peer received journals in different disciplines.

It includes online e-resources viz. Bibliographical and full text databases and also gateway portals. The important full text database and Bibliographical Databases are:

Full Text Databases

URL

1. http://www.pubs.acs.org/ - American Chemical Society (Thirty e-journals)
2. http://journalsonline.tandf.co.uk. - Taylor and Francis (1105 e-journals)
3. http://www.blackwellsynergycom - Blackwell (489 e-journals)

4. http://www.aip.org/	-	American Institute of Physics (18 e-journals)
5. http://arjournals.annualreviews.org	-	Annual Reviews (29 e-journals)
6. http://www.springerlink.com/	-	Springer & Kluwer journals (1217 e-journals)
7. http://www.scienceonline.org/	-	Science on-line (1 e-journal)
8. http://www.rsc.org/	-	Royal Society of Chemistry (23 e-journals)
9. http://www.aps.org/	-	American Physical Society (10 e-journals)
10. http://www.journals.cambridge.org/	-	Cambridge University Press (189 e-journals)
11. http://www.sciencedirect.com/	-	Elsevier Science (34 e-journals)
12. http://www.muse.jhu.edu/journals	-	Project Muse (222 e-journals)
13. http://www.portlandpress.com/	-	Portland Press pp/default.htm (4 e-journals)
14. http://www.nature.com/	-	Nature (1 e-journal)
15. http://www.jstor.org/	-	J-STOR (457 e-journals)

16. http://www.emeraldinsight.com - Emerald (28 e-journals)
17. http://www.search.eb.com. - Encyclopedia Britanica
18. http://www.iop.org.EJ - Institute of Physics (36 e-journals)

Bibliographical Database (Archival Database)

1. http://www.rsc.org/ - Royal Society of Chemistry (6 Databases)
2. http://www.web5s.silverplatter.com/ - Biological Abstracts webspirs/start.ws? (From 1969+ Continued)
3. http://web5s.silverplatter.com/webspirs/ - Mathscinet (AMS) start.ws? (1940+continued)
4. http://www.stnweb.cas.org/ - Chemical Abstract Service (1917 + continued)

Gateway

All libraries are applying online technologies of their sources and services. Digital libraries is a hybrid of the print and digital products and a gateway to online resources to exploit the digital collection locally, nationally and globally. There may be some problems with web search engines. It has provided to gateway particularly the subject gateway to access the digital objects.

Subject gateways are the internet services which support systematic resource discovery. They provide links to various types of resources, the objects, the site and the services provided. Subject Gateway is more popular in U.K. User can approach to commercial global search engines through it. User can use subject gateway more conveniently in subject libraries. Greenstein explained that the users of both services benefits from an understanding of the boundaries and contents of the information space they are accessing.

Gateway provide a list of resources which are pre-selected to meet the user's requirements. Resources are accessed by users via hyperlinks from the gateways, particularly the resources which are located out of the region. Gateway is a:

(a) Process of identification
(b) Filtering
(c) Description
(d) Classification
(e) Indexing

It is freely available via WWW. Many models are being practiced or implemented by the libraries for information systems to seems up internet based content. Digital library service are operated by information gateways and portals and facilitated by internet and also acting as one possible solution to the problem of information retrieval and quality control which will be more effective than other solutions such as:

(a) search engine
(b) metadata
(c) classification schemes
(d) content creation

Services includes:

(a) Access to complementary database
(b) Web indexes of sites
(c) Personalisation
(d) Current awareness
(e) Community building services-being developed in other internet services

Important Gateways

Subject Gateways started its operation in 1995 with initiative by UK and USA to developed web based databases called subject gateways or subject based gateway to access the scholarly informations relating to broad subject area e.g. Engineering, Physics, Medicine and Agriculture etc. Important Gateways are:

1. Social Science Information Gateway (SOSIG)
2. Edinburgh Engineering Virtual Library (EEVL)
3. Architecture Gateway
4. Medical Information Network Gateway
5. INFOMINE (USA)
6. SCOUT (UK)

Open source gateway access carefully and select open access scholarly material available freely on the internet which includes bibliographic reports, thesis, e-print, databases and primary portals and specialty search. You can browse open source by subject or by resource type.

Approach to e-Learning

e-Learning is approved to facilitate and enhance learning through both computer and communications technology. Such devices can include personal computers, CD-ROMs, Digital Television, PDA and Mobile phones. e-Learning components include Learning Management System or Learning Content Management System, content, collaboration, testing and assessment, skills and competency, e-commerce and internet video based learning.

There are many software's available for e-learning:

1. ***Open Sources***
   (a) A Tutor
   (b) Docebo LMS
   (c) Dokeos
   (d) Internet

(e) Moodle
(f) Site@School
(g) Word Evicle

2. ***Commercial Software***
(a) ANGEL Learning LMS
(b) e-Portfolio
(c) Blackboard
(d) e-College
(e) edu XVLE system
(f) Gradepoint
(g) Inquisiq
(h) Learn.com
(i) Learn exact
(j) Web CT

e-Learning and e-Society

Educational technology is a systematic way of designing, implementing and evaluating, learning and teaching. The teaching methodology and present day classroom management have to undergo major changes to cope up with the cyber age. e-Learning Global super highway has opened the teaching of courses over the web.

Library Consortium

Consortium mean association for specific purpose. Library consortium means association among group of libraries towards a common goal of library service.

The reason behind consortium is the knowledge explosion, population cluster, document explosion, dependence attitude of libraries, library limitation of finance, staff and language barrier.

The following are the characteristics of successful library consortia:

1. Valuable products and services

2. Cooperation among participating agencies
3. Stability in service
4. Regular finance
5. Flexibility in exchange programmes
6. Successful document delivery service
7. Competitive charges

Resource sharing concept has developed the idea of consortia in electronic field that has been initiated and adopted by European countries for the first time. OCLC has been the first effort made by Ohio college and at later stage developed as "online catalogue of college libraries". It helped libraries to serve the people by providing economical access to knowledge through innovation and collaboration. Other projects are VIVA of Virginia and OHIOLINK of Ohio. But consortia is not being taken to application in libraries so popularly as it has so many limitations:

(a) Exorbitant membership fees
(b) Slow Bureaucracy
(c) All libraries are not simultaneous users
(d) Security methods are not sufficient
(e) Inadequate pricing formula

Problems of Designing Hypermedia

World Wide Web plays the role of a universal medium in educational area, e.g.

(a) Online tutorials
(b) Teaching Strategies
(c) Forms of interaction

Hypermedia establish relations between man and computer for extensive learning. Computer has become the tool of the active user. In recent years, the role of networked, interactive hypermedia has become increasing important in educational and training activities with the growth of internet. Hypermedia is becoming a desktop reality in educational learning. There are two levels:

education field and the educator. The first is based on logical structure and the other provides the information contents. Textbooks have a logical order of contents/topics. Students progress is effected by material available. In hypertext systems, the concept of order is reduced. In the light of this logic hypermedia is designed keeping in view the access potentiality of a large database that is connected by type of media.

There are few theories and models which are under-standable in computer environment and advice the designer to design the hypermedia in best ways to organize, present and index multimedia information to maximize learning and knowledge construction by students.

Components

1. Presentation – It refers to the way the content is displayed i.e. colour, music and image.
2. Functional elements – It refers to what the user can do i.e. Search engine and Quizzes.

Hypermedia in learning

1. More knowledge can be made available to students, in more accessible forms.
2. Good teaching made more affordable that teaching productivity can be increased.
3. Positive re-enforcement for students can be provided more effectively and efficiently.
4. Learning may become more on demand and hence more motivated.
5. Rare events and conditions can be seen on film or in creation and compared one with another.

17
Modern Learning Centers and e-Learning

Knowledge Representation

The quantities of material stored in libraries, pose the problem of finding what you want among the stacks, so to speak. In some collections of information, the user is simply overwhelmed. Attempts have been made over the years to provide a way to find information conveniently, often based on the idea of organizing everything by subject. Often, this was a byproduct of the need to put books on shelves.

Whether knowledge representation can be discussed outside of language processing is unclear. Famous linguistic says that language constrains thought. They suggested that there would be cultural differences in the way that different peoples thought about things based on their languages. In this view there is no independent representation of abstract thought other than a linguistic expression. Most artificial intelligence researchers reject the Sapir-Whorf hypothesis. They believe that there is some kind of abstract knowledge representation in the brain, which is translated to linguistic form when we talk or write, but which could be represented directly in the right mathematical structure.

In practice, it seems unlikely that any single knowledge representation scheme will serve all purposes. The more detailed such a scheme is, the less likely it is that two different people will come up with the same place in it for the same document. And the less detailed it is, the less resolving power it has and the less use it is. Tom Landauer did a number of experiments on the ability of people to give names to concepts. They would ask people to associate a single word with a picture or a concept, for example, the idea of a command that tells you how much money you have spent in some computer system. In Landauer's experiments, people generated so many different words as answers to task like this that in order to get 85% coverage of the answers, you need six different words. Of course, many of those words are also answers to different tasks. Thus, asking people to label concepts does not produce unique and reliable answers. Even professional indexers do not produce entirely reproducible results.

The dream of perfect vocabulary is an old one, although it originated with a slightly different problem. Until the Renaissance, most scholars in. Europe wrote in Latin, and they could all read one another's books. With the rise of vernacular literature, scholars became unhappy about their inability to read anything they wanted. Since Latin had been abandoned, some of them thought that perhaps an artificial language would succeed as a common language for all serious thought.

Words and Thesauri

This is what most systems do today, and it seems adequate for many tasks. But words fail in two respects. First, there are often many words used to describe the same idea; users looking for *scanning* may not search for *facsimile* or *imaging*. This produces *recall failures;* material that should be found is not. Second, the same word can mean two different things in different contexts. Sometimes it is possible to sort out the meanings by knowing the part of speech of the word. It is possible to guess parts of speech fairly accurately without doing a complete syntactic analysis. Geoffrey Sampson and coworkers developed statistical methods based on the probabilities of certain word sequences. They started with two kinds of information:

(a) A dictionary that gives all the possible parts of speech each word might have.

(b) A corpus of parsed English giving the parts of speech of each word, from which probabilities of different sequences could be computed.

Then, given a sentence, they would make a list of the possible choices for each word and look for the selection that would give the best overall probability for the sentence.

Knowledge Structures

Artificial intelligence researchers have attempted to define formal knowledge languages, with the goal of permitting knowledge to be expressed with such detail that it can be manipulated automatically. As in indexing thesauri, a typical knowledge representation language will have a hierarchy of concepts and then store relationships between them. For example, animals might be grouped into the traditional Linnean hierarchy, giving us:

(a) animal

(b) mammal

(c) carnivore

(d) dog

(e) fido

Looking carefully at this, the relationship between "Fido" and "dog" is not really the same as that between "dog" and "mammal": is and subset are typical names for these two distinct semantic relationships, is a meaning that the object is a specific example or instance of the related concept, while subset means that the object or objects are restricted examples of the concept. Formal knowledge structures exist only in a few areas of research. Chemistry, for example, has an elaborate and complete system of substance names, but nothing similar for reaction names.

The relationships between items can be of varying degrees of complexity. Once one gets beyond the defining hierarchy, there are many obvious relationships that can be used in writing down information. To understand the use of such relationships, remember the relationships in MeSH. If one wishes to distinguish not just the question of whether a particular substance causes or cures a particular disease, but all possible relationships between nouns, a great many relationships might be needed. Virtually every verb in the language might be needed as a link name between substantives. Normally, a somewhat smaller set is used, since a knowledge representation structure is supposed to be something more systematized than a parse tree. Often they seem similar to the cases used in linguistics: agent, object, location and so on.

By organizing the nodes of an artificial intelligence (AI) language into a hierarchy, each fact can be stored at an appropriate level. Of course, life is not always so simple. In a knowledge representation language, one could easily write.

Translating all written English into a knowledge representation language requires, in principle, the need to disambiguate every ambiguity in the original text. Clearly, this is not practical. For many ambiguous sentences, the speaker has been willing to say something with an ambiguity because it is not worth the trouble to resolve it; it will make no difference to the listener. We are accustomed to ambiguity that can be resolved and that which cannot be resolved.

However, the designers of A/L systems do not necessarily need to imagine converting all of an English text into a knowledge representation language. Two choices are converting some of the knowledge of a text into the formal language, or writing the knowledge directly in the formal language, instead of in English. The conversion idea was perhaps pursued most ambitiously by Roger Schank and his students at Yale. They worked on what were first called "scripts" and then called "MOPs" (memory organization processes) and which represented certain standard scenarios for common situations.

The problem with machine learning was that computers lacked the more elementary parts of the knowledge that people have. For more than two decades Lenat and associates have attempted to encode everything from elementary biology to time series. They ran into several practical difficulties. One was that a great deal of skill in logic was needed to enter the knowledge;

despite a goal of entering very simple knowledge, it was not possible as originally hoped to use high school students to do it. Another difficulty was that different people entering similar concepts would choose different ways to do it, as has happened in other experiments of this sort. Most serious was Lenat's discovery time and again that the basic principles of CYCL, his knowledge representation language, had to be adjusted as new areas of knowledge were studied.

Hypertext

If it is not going to be easy to translate all text manually into formal language, is it possible to rely on specific links for specific document to document queries? This is the model of "trails" suggested by Vannevar Bush in 1945 Theodor (Ted) Nelson rejuvenated this idea in 1960 and coined the name *hypertext* for it. In a hypertext document collection, there are pointers from one place in the text to another. Hypertext links, as commonly used, are asymmetrical: there does not need to be a link in the reverse direction for each forward link. They are also modeless: all links are the same kind of link, rather than being labelled with types. There were various experiments with hypertext systems in the 1970s and 1980s. Perhaps the best known are the systems at Brown University (IRIS) which attempted to use hypertext for teaching courses, and the programming systems like Hypercard (Apple) and Notecards (Xerox). Hypertext was frustrating both to write and to read. In terms of writing, the author has great difficulties writing something if the user need not have read the paragraph immediately preceding the one being written. A world in which readers jump from one place to another is one in which the author never knows what the reader already knows, and it becomes difficult to carry through a logical argument. Brown found it very time-consuming to create their hypertext courses, and the students in the courses contributed less than the researchers expected.

The readers have the converse problem. They can easily get lost, and not know how to get back to something they have read. *Navigation* quickly became the big problem in hypertext, and it became commonplace for each hypertext document to have one page which functioned like a traditional tale of contents or index, providing pointers to every place in the hypertext and being pointed to be every page as well. That way, users always had a place to which they could return and from which they could find any other point in the text.

Half the articles were general interest and half were technical. Both the linear (traditional) and hypertext versions of the articles were read on the same computer screens. The students remembered more of what they read in a linear format, although the time taken to read either version was about the same. The students also preferred the linear version.

Despite these early difficulties, hypertext has now exploded on the world. Today's famous hypertext system, of course, is the Web. Created by Tim Berners-Lee at CERN in 1990, the Web as of April 2003 contained about 20 terabytes of material in some 2 billion documents, with perhaps 30 pointers on each Web page, or a total of 60 billion hypertext links. Much of the Web consists of organizations of other people's page: there are innumerable hot lists, bookmarks, and other ways of keeping track of what has been seen. There are also, of course, the search engines, and finding things on the Web is partly handled by search engines and partly by the hypertext links.

Part of both the glory and the frustration of the Web is that it has no maintenance organization whatsoever. Individuals add and delete things at will making it easy for material to appear but also for it to disappear. The ability of individuals to place what they want on the Web has also produced problems, since some Web users want attention for their pages and do things like place irrelevant words on their page to attract the attention of search engines. Libraries will have to try to decide which items are relevant and useful and which are not.

Web pages can not only appear without any organizational approval, but also can and do disappear. The average life of a URL was 45 days in 1996 and has now crept up to 100 days, and with such short lifetimes, the Web is full of pointers to files that no longer exist. This means that somebody who sees something good on the Web must make a judgment as to whether it is likely to still be there if it is wanted again. If it does not appear to be from a source such as a university library or other permanent organization, the only safe thing to do will be to copy it, given permission. Not all URLs are short-lived; Half of the URLs were still valid after four years. There's no inconsistency here: there are a large number of URLs that turn over very quickly and then some more that are long-lived, and what Spinellis found is that URLs cited in reports tend to be drawn from more durable pages.

Whether, in the long run, libraries can rely on hypertext links as a way of accessing information is doubtful. Unorganized and amateur indexing has been tried in the past with "author-assigned keywords" and such proposals and has been inadequate for complete coverage; a surprising fraction of published papers are never cited at all. Thus, sole reliance on volunteer-built hypertext may not be an adequate method of achieving general library coverage.

Various libraries have attempted to collect Web sites professionally and provide guidance and learning to users; such Web pages are often called "gateways". The creation of such sites is expensive: it costs as much or more to catalog a Web site as to catalog a book. Many Web sites lack the equivalent of a title page telling you the author and publisher name; the cataloger must search around for the information. And a normal library doesn't have to check back on each book in its catalog regularly to see whether it has changed this week.

If reliance on manual methods is not going to be enough for libraries for learning what can be done mechanically? In the SMART project, Salton introduced the idea of the vector space as a way of handling documents in retrieval systems. In vector space mathematics, each different word in a document can be viewed as a direction in a very-high-dimensional space. The number of dimensions is equal to the number of different words in the document collection. The strength of the vector in each direction is the number of times that word (since each word is one dimension) appeared in the document. Thus, each document can be viewed as a vector in this high-dimensional space; and the similarity of two documents can be judged by looking at the angle between the vectors. Documents on very similar subjects should have a large angle between their vectors.

Salton also considered the use of a thesaurus in this model. In this case, each word was replaced with the thesaurus category to which it belonged, and the number of dimensions was the number of categories rather than the number of different words. This still leaves, however, an enormous number of dimensions. And that large number of dimensions means that it is often going to be the case that a particular document will not be found in a search for a particular concept, because a related concept was used to describe the document.

Attempts were made over the years, to identify related terms on the basis of their overlaps in documents. Statistical methods for word associations looked for words which appeared together. In fact, early suggestions directed one to look not for words which actually occurred together, but for those which occurred with similar word neighborhoods. For example, if we imagine that all documents are spelled with either consistent British or American spelling, the words *airplane* and *aeroplane* will not appear together, and their synonymy will be missed; a searcher who asks for only one word will not find documents containing the other one. But both of these words will appear in documents containing words such as *jet, propeller, wing, rudder, cockpit,* or *carry-on*. Thus, their relationship could be detected.

Landauer and Littman realized that by obtaining a collection of documents in two languages, and performing the term/document overlaps using both languages, they could make vector spaces into which terms from each language could be mapped. This eliminated the need for manual construction of a bilingual concept thesaurus, although a translated collection was still needed to start the process.

An interesting subquestion is the determination of which language an unknown text is written in so that a system can decide what software to put it through. One would not wish to index French or German under the misunder-standing that they were English.

There are various techniques to solve this-by looking for specific words that are very frequent in a particular language, or by looking at the letter frequencies in the language. A short text in any language, however, may be missing particular cue words. However, there is a cheap trick that works well: given known samples of the different languages, append the unknown text to each sample and run any standard compression algorithm that detects repeated strings on the combination.

Another technique for finding information is based on what has been used before. There is strong clustering in citations, in photocopy requests, and in library circulation. Digitally it will become much easier to gather such information and use it. Clustering phenomena in library usage are well known. A few items get heavy use, and many more are not used at all. The average item in a large research library does not circulate in an average year; one suspects it is not touched. Typically, 80% of the circulation of books comes from 20% of the titles.

Links with User

Historically, specific links provided by users have been important in the use of libraries; they came in the form of literature references. This is the basis of citation indexing. For some years, Science Citation Index (from the Institute for Scientific Information), has indexed papers based o the other papers they reference. As an alternative to keyword-based indexing, this can often turn up quite different documents. On the Web, it is similarly possible to track through hypertext links to a given page.

Will usage-based searching be important in a libraries as well? Digitally, it is much easier to track usage of different items. As yet, there are no systems that say, "Show me things other people have overlooked". Such a system is called *community-rated* information. The idea here is that you can model the search you want to do by looking at what other people have done. This is the logic of "Anything Joe recommends, I will like", done mathematically and with a large set of people.

Documents

Writing, of course, made it possible to have a permanent version of information, and writing on papyrus, parchment, and paper (rather than carving on stone walls) made it possible to move texts from place to place. In the Middle Ages there was an active market in copying manuscripts and selling them; this market was taken over by printed books when they arrived.

The economies of scale in modern publishing are such that it is difficult to issue a book today in a small press run. University presses are pressured by authors who wish to see their books in print in order to get tenure; but their main market is university libraries, none of which have budget increases adequate to keep up with the inflation in book prices. Since so many of the costs of printing a book are incurred before the first copy comes off the press, a small press run means high costs, and thus high prices, which further cause libraries to reduce purchases.

Scholarly journals are even more affected by the push from authors to see their names in print. Their prices have been raised to levels that no one could have imagined 30 years ago; today a journal subscription can cost as much as a new car. The publishers react to statistics on the increasing costs facing libraries by pointing to the general consumer price index increase plus the increase in the number of pages per journal issue; together these effects dominate the journal price increases. The libraries, however, have no way of enforcing greater selectivity on the publishers to keep the sizes down, and there is a residual increase in inflation-adjusted price per page.

Traditional publishing and distribution have accelerated substantially in recent years. Time-to-maker is everything on instant books, and publishers have learned to speed up printing and distribution even for ordinary books. Libraries wishing to exchange items can take advantage of a wide array of new delivery services specializing in overnight package handling, and of course the fax machine has made interlibrary copying of journal articles a very rapid process.

The greatest recent change in book distribution has been the great increase in the variety of titles available to the average reader. The rise of the chain bookstores, with enormous stores replacing smaller, individual booksellers, was the first step; then came Amazon.com and its competitors, offering essentially every book in print.

CD-ROM has become a popular media in publication field particularly in the period in the early 1990. CD-ROMs share many distribution properties with books. The CD manufacturing process, like the book publishing process, is most economical at large production runs. It was designed for high-run popular music disks, and the signal can be read as digital or converted to analog sound. CD-ROMs cost, in quantity, much less than a book. Their distribution began in the mid 1980s, some half dozen years after the audio CD started. Through the late 1980s, some half dozen years after drives and began to purchase

CD-ROM versions of the abstracting and indexing journals. These purchases displaced online searching on a pay-per-minute basis; libraries realized that if they were spending large amounts of money on online searching, they could save money by purchasing the same database on CD-ROM.

Soon most databases started appearing CD-ROM, which pushed out magnetic tape and competed effectively with the very expensive online services then common. Then, in the early 1990s, the individual CD-ROM business exploded. CD-ROM drives dropped in price at the same time that software distributors realized they wanted to distribute much larger programs. When PC computer RAM memory was limited to 640K, a 1.4MB diskette was an adequate distribution mechanism. Now that PCs with 500 MB of internal memory are common and software comes with manuals, options, and elaborate background images, we cannot deliver software in units of 1.4 MB. Many CD-ROMs came on to the market, with the market doubling every year up to early 1995, including in particular the home reference market. CD-ROM encyclopedias more or less destroyed the market for print encyclopedias. Other important categories of reference CD-ROM publishing were atlases, phonebooks, and educational aids for children.

CD-ROM publishing was unusually concentrated by the standards of normal publishing. The distribution channels were harder to break into than for books; stores sold relatively few titles and most of those were from a few major publishers (most obviously Microsoft). Unlike audiobooks, which are sold in normal bookstores, CD-ROMs are sold largely through computer stores, which don't have the same traditions of special orders and generous stocking policies. Consumers got tired of CD-ROM books rather quickly as the Web became available, and the CD-ROM market collapsed.

18
Computer Networks

The learning centers allows much faster alternatives to faxes or postal mail for sharing information between libraries. Computer networks now link almost every country in the world. Of course, computers have always exchanged bits with their peripheral devices. These exchanges typically follow a protocol in which one device is in charge and the other is responding. A key difficulty in designing intercomputer protocols, and part of the reason why they are different from protocols used within a single computer, is that they must anticipate that the two machines are of equal status; neither can be assumed willing to just wait around for the other one. Also, of course, the longer delays involved in transmitting over distances and through phone lines means that the protocols cannot assume immediate responses to all messages. The winning network has turned out to be the Internet, running IP (the Internetworking protocol).

There are several basic choices to be made in network design. These include the choice of packet or circuit switching, and the choice of bus or star physical arrangements. In a packet network, each batch of information is handled separately. The analogy is postal mail or the telegram; in fact, packets are often called datagrams. Packet networks are like adding soil to your garden, bucket by bucket. In a circuit network there is a preliminary negotiation to set up a route and then information flows along it. An analogy is the telephone system or the way that water flows along a hose; the faucets are turned and then the water moves. Roughly speaking, a circuit network involves overhead to arrange a path, but may recover the cost of the arrangements by being able to move information faster. A packet network is simpler since each packet is completely independent, but there is no opportunity to save routing arrangements that have been set up for one packet to use for future ones.

To run wires around a building, two different topologies can be used. One wire can be threaded through each place that needs one, and everything hung off that wire, like the lights on a Christmas tree. This is called "bus" wiring: one wire passes every place that needs service. The alternative is to have each spot that needs a wire connected to a central location, like a fusebox, for example. This is called "star" wiring since a map of the wires looks like a star, with lines going from one central point to each spot that needs service.

Bus wiring requires less total wire, but requires everybody to share the same wire. It is thus appropriate for a system in which expensive but high-capacity wire is used. Some early computer networks relied on coaxial cable and leaned towards bus wiring. However, bus wiring creates some administrative problems. Since everyone is sharing the same physical cable, if one machine on the cable malfunctions, everyone may suffer loss of service. Similarly, a cable break necessarily affects a great many users. Thus, there has been a tendency to use star wiring, made of cheaper wires, but meaning that each machine has its own connection to some kind of data closet or local switch. This kind of system is easier to manage and usually cheaper to install and-in the form of the 10-base-T standard using twisted pairs of copper wire-has replaced the thick coaxial cable Ethernet. It also simplifies administration of the network, since users are less likely to interfere with each other.

Wireless networks are now coming to prominence. Each computer has a radio antenna, transmitter, and receiver; thus, even though there is no cost for "wire", the network is likely to be more expensive in hardware than a wired network. However, installation is much easier, with no holes to be drilled in walls or cables to be run. Wireless networks, like bus networks, can be overloaded or interfered with by one user. And, like a bus network, one user can overhear the packets transmitted by other users. Wireless is thus a kind of bus.

This extremely simple Aloha protocol cannot use much of the bus throughput, since as usage increases, the chance increases that two computers will transmit at once. One improvement was the so-called slotted Aloha in which transmission occurs at fixed intervals, instead of transmitting at will. Ethernet improved this further while relating the passive medium of Aloha. The Ethernet fabric is a plain coaxial cable with no active parts, and thus fewer chances to fail. As in Alohanet, machines communicate by putting addressed packets on the bus fabric. What Ethernet adds is the idea that machines listen as they are transmitting. If, before it starts sending, a computer hears some other machine transmitting, it does not transmit. And, should two machines start transmitting so closely together in time that neither hears the other before starting to send, they both stop as soon as they detect the collision. Each then waits a random time before trying again, so that the next try will not produce a collision detection). It is still not possible to use all the capacity of the cable, but it is a great improvement over the original Alohanet. In the Ethernet protocol, each machine needs to be able to hear every other machine in a time shorter than that required to transmit an entire packet. This limits a single Ethernet to perhaps 100 meters, depending on the transmission speed on the cable.

The simplicities of the basic Ethernet idea are sometimes disadvantages. Every machine can see every packet on the cable, no matter to whom it is addressed. Unless packets are intended for them. Also, there are no constraints on the ability of an individual machine to transmit. If a machine on the cable goes haywire and starts transmitting constantly, ignoring all collisions and all other machines, there is nothing the other machines can do. Fortunately, a single Ethernet is limited in length and is likely to be contained within a singly administered domain, so something can be done to bring pressure on the operator of the haywire machine to fix it or at least shut it down.

Since a single Ethernet is only 100 meters long, Ethernets have to be connected to build larger networks. At first, this can be done by bridges which simply sit between to cables and copy every packet from one of them onto the other one. This doubles the traffic on the cables, however, and is not an adequate answer for large networks. Larger networks need routers. A router is a device that sits between two networks and, like a bridge, moves packets from one to another. But a router does not move every packet across the network. It knows which addresses are on which side. In the simple one-bus Ethernet, machines can be very sloppy about addresses because as long as each sender and receiver know who they are, it doesn't matter if any other machine does. Once routers are introduced, however, addressing matters. Each router looks at each packet address and decides whether it belongs only on the cable it came from or should be sent to a different cable.

What does a router do if it wants to put a packet on an Ethernet cable but suffers a collision? It must wait and try again, just like a normal computer. And this means it must have some memory to save up packets which it has to retransmit. Packet networks with routers are thus store-and-forward networks in which information flows with somewhat unpredictable timing towards the destination.

Of course, a network with routers in it is no longer totally passive. Nevertheless, the basic notion that computer networks have a cheap, dumb fabric and intelligent devices persists, and contrasts with the idea of the telephone network as containing expensive switches and dumb telephones as peripheral devices. In 1996 a digital telephone switch cost about Rs.1600/- line (world average price) and the phones were Rs.1200/- and at later stage these prices revisited (2003) and found carriers quoting average costs of Rs.9000/- to Rs.12000/- phone line/year for analog circuit switched service. By contrast, hubs and routers connect high priced computers, and the Ethernet card, if not included, costs may be Rs.2000/-. The cost of the hubs and routers is down to Rs.700/- per line. The central cost of the traditional telephony service is much higher than that for data switching, and nowadays even the distributed cost of the data switching is lower. Stringing the wire, now the same unshielded twisted pair for either voice or data, is more expensive: wiring may cost Rs.4000/- per line within a typical building.

The real precursor of the networks we have today was the Arpanet, started in 1969 by Larry Roberts. Arpanet was a connection between computers doing military research and was provided to these sites by the Department of Defense. ARPA was then the Advanced Research Projects Agency of the Department of Defence; it's now DARPA, with Defense added to the acronym. The Arpanet was high-speed: it started with 56K lines at a time when 300 baud modems were still standard. Arpanet was intended from the beginning to be real-time, since it was to support remote computing facilities so that users at RAND could log into computers at MIT or at military bases.

Over the years, more and more machines joined the Arpanet. Fewer and fewer of the institutions running these machines had military research as their primary purpose; at the same time, the military was starting to use the Arpanet for more critical applications than research and became less comfortable about sharing the net with other users. In the mid-1980s, the Arpanet was split and divided into MILNET, a purely military set of machines, and the civilian machines. NSF took over the administrative and funding responsibility for the backbone of the civilian networks, called NSFNET. NSFNET connected the key supercomputer centers and other users bridged into those centers. The funding NSF provided was relatively small but enabled the backbone to stay up without complex ways of allocating its costs.

As traffic on the Internet exploded in 1994 and 1995, more and more commercial companies started connected customers to the NSFNET backbone. Since NSF had a goal of supporting researches and for years maintained an "acceptable use policy" which limited what the commercial organizations were allowed to do on the net, the commercial organizations began building their own backbones, and as a result the Internet is no longer receiving NSF support. This change was transparent to most users, as the commercial companies interchange traffic without regard to which one of them owns the link to the end consumer.

Most libraries are now connected to the Net, as are most schools. As the costs of Internet connection decline, the actual connection is much less of a question than the need for staff that knows what to do with it. Libraries are also, in some communities, seeking the role of providing Internet access to people who do not have their own connection at home. Within most advanced countries, however, the spread of Internet connectivity into homes is moving so fast that there will be little role for libraries to do this.

Noll in 1991 suggested that voice telephony would dominate into the indefinite future. In fact, the Internet and data traffic are now larger than voice telephony traffic; data traffic first took the lead on international links, especially trans-Pacific but data traffic passed voice even within 2002. Internet telephony is now common: witness the use of packets to transmit ordinary voice calls. This is called VoIP (Voice over Internet Protocol, or more commonly Voice over IP). Many people aren't even aware they are using it; they buy prepaid phone cards and have no idea that the vendor is using the Internet and packets to handle their international call.

Information on the Internet

The two original services were remote login and file transfer. These have since been encapsulated so that the user does not perceive what is being done, but the basic rules are the same: a user connects to a machine (called a server), and then bits are transferred to the user's remote machine (the client).

The earliest service was remote login. Here, all the computing and data are actually on the server machine. Effectively, the client machine is merely a remote terminal. It has no computing to do other than to provide the screen display, and it need have no copies of the data being transmitted. Often, however, the user wishes to obtain actual data fields from the server machine and keep these. For example, the server may not be providing catalog access, but may be providing a library of "freeware" software or freely available text that users may be welcome to download. For file transfers, the standard protocol was ftp (file transfer protocol). Quite large arrays of information became available on some servers using ftp, including, for example, the literature texts held by Project

Gutenberg, the software distribution at many sites, collections of images posted by people, and many other kinds of information. Inherently, ftp involves people making copies of files, resulting in problems distributing updates and old versions proliferating around the world.

The ftp interface was not easy to use, and widespread acceptance had to await the gopher system from the University of Minnesota. The gopher interface was based on the concept of hierarchical menus and was text-only. It was overrun by the Web and the browsers: first by Mosaic, designed by Marc Andreesen (then at the National Center for Supercomputer Applications at the University of Illinois) and later by Netscape and then Internet Explorer.

Another option with browsers is the use of links in Web pages, which is unconstrained. As in the tradition of hypertext, anybody can put a link to anything. The collection of all such pages is called, of course, the World Wide Web, and Web pages can be found in virtually all the ways described so far.

- There are free-text search engines that retrieve everything on the Web at regular intervals and index it; Google is the best known.
- There are lists, arranged by subject, of pages on particular topics; the best known are those of Yahoo (yet another hierarchical organization) and AOL.
- There are hypertext pointers on most pages, creating a great chain of references which can be followed.

The longer-range hope that Web browsing might be turned over to "agents", which operate in the user's place. These agents would do searching, retrieval, and display of information which the user might want. As a simple example, an agent might understand different protocols, such as the formats of documents in PDF or Word or La Tex, and invoke the correct "viewer" as needed. Most Web browsers already do something like this. More complex agents might maintain standing queries to run against news sites every day and forward interesting stories; again, this is a service readily available from portals. Someday, the marketers hope, agents will shop for you, maintain your calendar, and schedule your entertainment. How accurately they can do this and how much they will be distorted by commercial advertising is not yet clear.

Essentially, every Learning Centre today is on the Web. It is the standard way for distributing material and it is what everyone expects. Today, a service with its own non-Web interface would be considered unusual and frighten off users. Even if your digital library is going to have a peculiar and idiosyncratic access method, it will almost certainly be wrapped in a Web page. Online book catalogs, for example, often predated the Web and used "telnet" or "gopher" as their interfaces, but have nearly all become Web pages. The Web is now the overall space of online information; learning centres are specific collections within that space.

Grid Computing

The largest computation jobs these days are not done by single supercomputers, but by collections of smaller machines. In fact, even the architecture of a supercomputer today is likely to be that of multiple processors, rather than a single super-fast device. What does vary is the distance between the machines and their administrative control.

(a) Sometimes there are single, giant boxes, which contain thousands of processors. These are correctly called supercomputers even though no individual processor is that much faster than what you can buy in a desktop. Such machines now dominate the commercial supercomputer business, having replaced the machines that one hoped different kinds of electronics would give the main advantage.

(b) Sometimes there are multiple boxes, but connected locally and under the control of one administrator. The most common architecture for these is called "Beowulf", and the machines can either be bought or locally designed.

(c) Sometimes the machines are all over the world and the problem is parceled out. Each machine gets a bit of the problem and reports back its result over the Internet. There need not be any common management or administration of the machines.

The general idea of using large numbers of machines with loose connections to attack big problems is called "grid computing". We don't have a good understanding of which problems can be subdivided easily and attacked this way, as opposed to which problems can be subdivided easily and attacked this way, as opposed to which problems really required a more tightly bound architecture. In addition to issues of efficiency, there is a problem of trust vandals might attempt to subvert a large computation by sending in inaccurate results. In some problems, it is easy to check what is being reported; more generally, each subproblem has to be assigned multiple times.

Digital libraries use multiple computers typically for storage, not computation. A library can protect against loss of information by sharing its files with another library so that any files lost through a head crash, fire, earthquake, or erasure, whether accidental or malicious, can be retrieved from the other site. This sort of task raises the same issues of trust and organization that sharing cycles requires. So far, most libraries have only stored their copies on computers belonging to other libraries; although there is a lot of empty disk space on desktops, we don't have a "preserve your library at home" group, partly because disk space is not so cheap that we don't really need it.

e-Book

In addition to networked computing, information can be distributed by putting it on special-purpose handheld devices. During 2000 there was a brief flurry of interest in the "e-book", the idea that people would read full books on special purpose machines. Online reading of whole books had not been popular, and among the reasons given was lack of portability. So a few startups explored the idea of selling a device that somebody could carry around and read from, downloading books into it. Others worked with the pocket organizers (PalmPilots, PocketPCs, and their ilk) to provide books for reading on these devices.

In general, this was a failure. The publisher ventures, such as AtRandom, MightyWords, or iPublish, have largely folded up. Is this a fundamental problem, or a marketing issue? Are people not interested in reading from screens? Are the screens not quite good enough yet? Was the content not interesting enough? Or is it a question of price and availability?

Certainly, the small size of the screens made many books less convenient than paper, along with issues of lighting and battery life. Late in 2002, Microsoft announced the "Tablet", trying to see if a screen size more like that of an ordinary sheet of paper would be more attractive to users that a conventional laptop or pocket organizer. At least as of summer 2004, this does not seem to have made a significant different, obviously, a larger machine introduces a penalty in size, weight, and battery life which offsets the gains in readability.

Some of the marketing practices of the e-book companies undoubtedly discouraged customers. There is a tradition of providing a device cheap in order to sell the consumable it needs later-historically, shaving company made its money on blades, not razors. Thus the e-book companies would not subscribe to standard formats, but tried to force the user to buy all their e-books from one vendor. Prices were typically comparable to those of paperback books. The selection of material available from publishers varied widely.

Will we see a revival of handheld reading devices? Screens are still getting cheaper and better, and we're learning how to extend battery life. Someday, we should have devices that are comparable in weight and readability to a sheet of paper, and which will still have the advantages that one can search the book one is reading, or store many thousands of books in one device. But, at that time, it is also likely that the general-purpose Web browser will be a similar device; all it will take is a wireless connection in addition to the screen, memory, and CPU. So why would somebody want to buy a special-purpose device just for reading a particular book format?

Perhaps the marketers can come up with a package that gives the reader access to a wide selection of published material at a reasonable price, without the user feeling like an unwilling captive of some "book dealership". If so, we might see a revival of the handled electronic book, but I am skeptical. I suspect that generally accessible Web services with some way to buy current publications will arrive first.

Computer Connectivity

Is it safe to put information on the Web, or even to connect a computer to it? Computer viruses and computer crime have given a bad reputation to many kinds of computer connections, and the Web is no exception. Fortunately, the kind of viruses that infected MS-DOS computers and are based on special file extensions on diskettes are not email which turns into an executable file and wreaks havoc-relevant to most Web programming. However, the presence of servers that respond to outside commands does offer possibilities to vandals and criminals, and Web servers need to be careful about the steps taken to protect their programs. Users are now accustomed to seeing messages that ask them to download and install some particular viewer program in order to see some particular Web page; it is important that these programs be trustworthy in order to preserve computer files. There is no substitute for basic security and sensible administration on the server machines. Each user should have a password, and each password should be checked to see that it is not easily guessed (i.e. that it is not a common English word or name, or obvious string of letters). Each user should have a separate password, and each reminded to keep it private. There are many administrative decisions to be made which enforce security. For example, at one point, a major workstation manufacturer was shipping machines configured so that any remote machine could log in without any authorization check. Reasonable systems administrators would change this configuration before connecting the machine to the Internet.

In this context, it is important to remember that in line with the general behavior of Ethernets, it is possible for people to snoop on nets and collect packets. They can then look through these packets with programs for login and password sequences, or numbers that appear to be credit cards, and attempt to misuse them. This is not as bad as, say, cellphone conversations, where (as the British royal family found out to its discomfort) there are so many people spending their spare time listening to scanners that perhaps half of all cellphone conversations are overhead. But it does pose risks against which server operators should protect themselves.

One obvious danger comes from the telnet connections, which allow outsiders to log in. Computer vandals regularly probe machines on the Internet looking for chances to log in to the computers, trying various names and passwords that have been found by evavesdropping or by other means. Telnet has now been abandoned by many organizations in favor of *ssh*, "secure shell", which does not transmit passwords in the clear. Another protection is the use of firewalls to separate machines from the outside Web.

A firewall machine is simply another server computer which bridges packets between the outside Net and the computers inside an organization; it is a kind of router. It decides which packets to let through based on various principles and authorization rules. For example, it may allow only connections to the http port, except for authorized users. The trick is to decide whether someone sending in packets is indeed an authorized user. Relatively little information comes with the packets that is of use; in particular, the identification of the sending machine cannot be relied on, since it is possible to send messages with fake identification. One feature that a firewall router should have is a little bit of knowledge about possible sources of packets, and it should reject packets that are obviously mislabelled as to their origin (e.g., if they are labelled as coming from a machine inside a corporation but have appeared on the outside of the firewall).

The simplest way to verify the legitimacy of a packet source is a password. The problem with passwords that do not change is that if a vandal snoops on the net and picks up a password today, the vandal can use it tomorrow. Attempts to print out a sequence number for each logon or the date of the last logon, hoping that the legitimate user will notice if these are wrong, are not really reliable. Thus, good systems rely on identification strings that are never used twice. Two such schemes are the SecurID cards marked by Access Control Encryption, Inc., and the S/Key system invented at Bellcore.

The SecurID card is a credit-card-sized computer with battery, clock, and a display window that shows a six-digit number. Inside the card, an algorithm computes a new six-digit number every minute. The company supplies a program for the firewall machine that can run the same algorithm and thus know for each card what number it should be displaying at any time. A user identifies the card (not using any number printed on the outside) and enters the six digits it is displaying; the firewall compares this number with what it should be, and, if they match, the user must really be in possession of that card.

User Needs

Despite the widespread acceptance of the content and searching in libraries today, the match to what users actually want and what they can do is very weak. Users are neither clear about what they want, able to operate the systems well, or doing much to get help. However, they're satisfied with the results. To the extent that we can tell, the acceptance of new systems is partly based on the inability of users to tell how badly things are actually working, and partly on the probability that older systems were also not being used very effectively. At least, we have opportunities for improvement, if we can pay enough attention to the users when designing the systems.

Despite jokes about librarians who think their job is to keep the books safe from the readers, libraries exist to provide information to people, today and in the future. Digital libraries also provide information and services to their users. How will those services change and what new things will be happening?

Traditional libraries provided services that extended from entertainment to advanced research, but did not cover as wide a range as that on the Web. For example, libraries often rented videotapes, but rarely encouraged patrons to use library television sets and VCRs to watch them on the premises. Libraries could feasibly provide daily newspapers for financial and weather information with 24-hour delay, but do not have current stock tickers or weather reports. On the other hand, as compared with the Web, libraries have librarians who can help users with their requests, and they provide a range of services to children (such as reading aloud to them) which are not realistic or practical online.

We have a model of the "information seeking" user in which the user has an "information need" of some kind, which is then expressed in some form of query, and then receives an answer in the form of a citation to some document. The user then reads the document and decides whether and how to rephrase the query. Once upon a time the user might have looked in some paper index, such as *Reader's Guide to Periodical Literature*, and found a list of traditional bibliographic citations; nowadays, the query goes to Google and the user gets a set of URLs, which are easier to turn into real documents. The user might also approach a reference librarian with the query, and the librarian might use a variety of sources, both print and digital, as well as personal memory and experience, to suggest a list of possible answers.

However, this model is oversimplified. Often, the result of seeing a possible list of answers is not just a change in the way the information need is expressed, but a change in the original need itself. In addition, many queries are really very vague and fuzzy. Although half the people in a library enter with a particular item in mind that they want to find, the majority of the people who walk into a public branch library or browse the racks at an airport bookstall are just looking for something interesting to read; they have no particular book in mind.

Even to the extent that people can describe something that they want, often the description is not in a form that lends itself to description in keywords for either Google or a printed index. Qualities such as the language of the text or the place or date of publication are often in catalogs and may be supported by a search engine or OPAC (online public access catalog). Some additional qualities are imaginable as catalog contents: the user might want a short book, or a children's book, or an illustrated book, or a popularization as opposed to a book for experts. Often people say that they remember the color or shelf position of a book they want to find; regrettably, their memory is often wrong or at least insufficiently precise to be a useful search term (and of course shelf position can change over time, whether in a library, bookstore, or home).

Access for Learning

The primary user service in the traditional library is access to books journals, but most libraries also provide reference services, circulation, catalogs, photocopying, and simple study space. More elaborate services can include interlibrary loan, reading aloud to children, training classes, sound and video collecting, maintaining book reserves, running book sales, advice to tourists, running exhibitions, and more. The user population is usually defined in some way, whether residents of a particular town or students, faculty, and staff at some educational institution. However, enforcement of entry requirements is often minimal, the main reason for library cards being the need to keep track of those who borrow books. Typically, even in some large university libraries, anyone is allowed to walk in and browse (many state universities must, by law, admit every citizen for on-site services). Geography is enough to see that almost every user of a typical library will be somebody from the community which is paying for it.

Libraries have a corresponding but changed list of activities. Access can be larger and broader, with no need to limit collecting by shelf space. Circulation is unnecessary for Web access, since, in general, no physical copies of anything are being circulated. There are some services, such as Netlibrary, which do manage their materials on a simultaneous use basis. This kind of analogy to traditional borrowing lets each copy be read by only one user at a time; each user in turn gains access to the digital file for a time set by the library and then "returns" it so that some other reader may read it. The library can buy as many "copies" of each book as are needed to provide for simultaneous readers. The loaning of physical "e-books" may also involve a more traditional circulation.

More challenging problems are the provision of reference and help services. For those users in the library, it is much as before; but many of the users of a digital library service are not physically present and may be continents and hours away. Libraries offer telephone, email, and online chat alternatives; they even make arrangement with libraries around the world so that someone with a problem in the middle of the night in one place can try to get assistance from someplace in an appropriate time zone. For example, Global Librarian is a collaboration of libraries in the United Kingdom, Canada, and Australia; somewhere in this list, it is likely to be normal operating hours. However, it's impossible to provide the same degree of encouragement or service to those not on the premises.

Librarians were attracted to microfilm since a relatively cheap photographic process produced enormous space reductions and also a "user copy" that could be employed in place of fragile originals. Newspapers were particularly appropriate for film, since they were bulky, printed on volatile paper, and the combination of large size and weak paper meant that they were particularly likely to tear or be damaged by heavy use. What went wrong with microfilm? Technically, it works just fine, but in every library microfilm readers sit idle while computer terminals have to have time limits. Let's take a look at the pluses and minuses of microfilm in contrast to the Web. We'll start with the downside. Disadvantages of microfilm include:

1. Microfilm has no full-text search capability. A few things can be bar coded, but at most this usually gives you access to a frame number. Readers have the tedious job of paging through, frame by frame.
2. Microfilm requires visiting the library. You can't do it from your office or home.
3. Microfilm readers are often difficult to use, and in actual practice are often broken (partly because so many of the

readers are unfamiliar with them and do not know how to use them), and sometimes produce either headache, eyestrain, or backache as a result of the chairs and lighting conditions available. Film (or fiche), especially older photography, can be difficult to read.

4. Material on microfilm is usually not as up to date as even printed material, since normally it takes at least a few months from the time something is printed until the microfilm edition is shipped (if only because a number of issues of the journal or paper have to be collected). For those interested in timely information, microfilm won't do.

5. One microfilm can only be read by one person at a time; digital copies can be read simultaneously by many. This is rarely a problem, given the low use of most filmed publications; and of course what is listed here as an advantage of digital is considered a disadvantage by publishers.

Advantages of microfilm include:

1. Microfilm contents are, in a way, twice-selected at least for those microforms which are alternative versions of print publications (as opposed to films of original manuscripts or business records). This material was originally chosen for publication, and then it was selected for filming rather than just discarding. Thus, it's usually reliable and high-quality information.

2. Microfilm is known to be durable and accepted as a long-term preservation medium. This is more interesting to the librarians rather than the users.

Similarly, we could look at the CD-ROM versions of publications which flourished through the late 1980s and early 1990s. Like microfilm, CD-ROMs saved shelf space and avoided damage to paper originals. However, they share many of the disadvantages of microfilm. The user must go to the library to use them; a special machine is required; and often no search capability can be offered (since many early CD-ROMs were just page images of the printed version). Again, CD-ROMs are losing out to online database.

Library Materials

Comparing the combination of card catalog and shelf browsing with the modern electronic full-text search, certainly we can find content more accurately, but not necessarily style or genre. The question of what kinds of queries users have, of course, varies not only with the users but also with the library system and the user experience. Users will learn to ask queries that they have found can be answered. Further, users choose which library to go to depending on what they want; there is little point in going to a research archive if you want a children's book or to a science library if you want literary commentary.

Users normally have a process in mind. They start with some kind of query, but then they change it as they do searches. System designers tend to think of isolated queries, each one to be answered and then forgotten. Designers assume that the users have read and understood the instructions so that they know whether or not the system does suffixing, whether they are searching a formal controlled vocabulary or ordinary words, and so on. In fact, users often do not know these things and often don't even know these issues exist, so they don't approach a librarian for help.

By contrast, 90% of the searches done with reference librarians are successful, although again the users often start with a problem statement that is much too broad. The librarian, however, shows the user sample books, talks through the issues, and almost always comes up with a suitable problem statement and response. It doesn't matter as much exactly what the librarian asks, rather than the librarian shows interest and elicits additional information from the user.

19

Development of Libraries and Learning Centers in the Development of Learning and Thinking in Ancient and Medieval India

If anybody wants to know the present, he should have the knowledge of the past. The study of the historical growth and development produces principles, which are valid because they make the relations contained in the subject explicit. Understanding the past experiences uncovers the meaning of present situations and thereby provides us the definite criteria for selecting what is relevant and in deciding what is important for the education or libraries? It is necessary to know the libraries of ancient and medieval times, their aims and objectives and how they were organized and administered, so as to enable us to get a clear perspective of the present day library systems. These studies will reveal that some of the tools, techniques and methods of ancient and medieval libraries, borne by traditions and practice have continued in those of modern libraries and they have profited them. Besides enquires and methods, practices and organizations of ancient and medieval libraries may furnish us the better insight into social and cultural life of the people of those days.

Development of Libraries and Learning Centers

Libraries are said to be the cultural signpost of any country. Commenting upon the importance of the libraries, Prof. Gates says:

(a) Libraries are essential ingredients of a civilized society.

(b) Libraries come into being to meet certain recognized needs.

(c) Certain conditions whether economic, social, scientific and cultural, encourage the development of libraries.

As far as the development of libraries is concerned, it is closely related with the development of civilization. The most ancient record of library starts from the inscription, which is also the oldest record of civilization itself. On the basis of present records and knowledge, it can be said that the Sumerians were first people who developed the writing system. It is evident from the history that Sumerians were fond of libraries as they established many private religious libraries. Babylonians were the neighbours of the Sumerians. There was not much difference in the style of writing in between them. Babylonians also had many libraries in their temples. The library of Borsippa was the most important library at that time, but now no authentic evidence is available regarding the holdings of that library. Later Assyrians and Egyptians civilization flourished well. But the writing techniques of Egyptians were well ahead than the Babylonians and Assyrians. King Asurbanipal of Assyria, who lived during 668 to 626 BC, developed a good library at Nineveh. A number of libraries were also developed in Egypt. Among them, the Library at Gizeh and the Library at Thebes around 250 BC are most famous libraries. Polycrates, the tyrant of Samos and Pisistratus, the tyrant of Athens established two Royal Libraries in Greece during 6th century. The libraries developed and established in Alexandrian period, are also famous.

During the Roman period, libraries were made open to the public. Though these were much restricted, books being chained to the cases. Community of learned men increased rapidly and multiplied the number of books. Prior to the invention of printing technology, the manuscript libraries were restricted both in the forms and the contents for the scholars. Kings and the emperors maintained their libraries as symbol of their privilege in the society. Highlighting the society conditions, *Al-Baruni* writes that women and girls were able to read, write and understand the Sanskrit.

They learned to play, dance and paint portraits. Though no sharp line can be drawn to indicate a decline and appearance of ancient and medieval libraries, the difference is only the uses of Parchment codex. The contribution of monk-houses in the development of libraries and the literacy during medieval period is also praiseworthy. A number of monks were engaged to copy the manuscripts.

In the age of renaissance, the public became more inquisitive. Around fifteenth century, scholars started to bring literature from the libraries from monasteries of Latin classic. During his period, the collection of books was honoured as wealth. The use of books became wider and the prince's libraries became more or less open. Mohammedan invasions on India, marked the beginning of momentous changes not only in social and political sphere but also in the domain of education and learning. After the advent of Islam in India, Muslims wanted to keep the impact of Islam in the way of life but the Hindus had no desire to be influenced by the Muslims. Muslim culture were profound and far reaching when Arabs came to India. The Arabs learned from the Hindus a great deal in the practical art of administration.

Education System

The method of instruction was oral in ancient time. Learning through memory served the purpose of quick, relevant and authentic information. It was said that *Sruti* or *Veda* should appeal to the ears not the eyes and the *Srutis* were not to be reproduced to writings. The methods of teaching were meant more to rouse the disciples to mental activities rather than to instruct them into dogma. Some mnemonics devices were employed to ease memorizing. The tone high or low, the gestures, signs and the symbols, of course not recorded any where, were used in giving lessons. Consequently the memory of the learned was the storehouse of knowledge.

Centers of Learning

There were *Brahmans* who were engaged in learning. The *Ashrams* of the great sages were also the centers of learning. This system of education was known as Gurukula System and it continued till Christian era, when organized educational institutions came to be evolved. Then came into existence, the Hindu temple colleges and Buddhist monastic universities. Every educational colony had within itself an academy of learned and religious men called *Parishad*. The *Parishad* was constituted of at least ten *Brahmanas*. There were also hermitages situated on the banks of rivers. The students gathered round the teachers from far and near. During the Christian era the *Ghatika* was a renowned center of learning. The temples were the centers of learning and they worked as main stays of Hinduism.

Takshashila and Other Libraries

Takshashila was the ancient city near Rawalpindi (now in Pakistan) around 700 BC. It was a center of Buddhist faith and in its library holdings perishable writing materials were used. Another library was *Valabhi* in 240-185 AD having literature on Buddhist faith. Other libraries were *Nalanda* of Eastern India, *Kanchipuram* of South India, and *Dhankataka* of Central India. It is believed that *Chanakaya* has also studied in the *Takshashila* University. *Takshashila* University was the most famous seat of learning. *Nalanda*, seven miles to the North-West of Rajgir (Patna) was the library and seat of learning of Buddhists. There were about 10,000 students in *Nalanda* University. The world-renowned teachers like *Nagarjuna, Vasubandhu, Viradeva, Chandragomin, Kanalasila, Sibbhadra* were there. The university was having a very good library, which had a huge building meant for higher studies in Buddhism. Probably, *Sakraditya* founded *Nalanda* library in 425 AD. *Balaputra Deva* the Kind of Sumatra and Java offered land and grants for construction of its library building. The library was called *Dharmaganga* having theology collection therein.

Vikramshila, a town near Bhagalpur (Bihar) was known for its monastic center established in abot 810 AD. It had a wonderful library established by Magadh King, *Dharampala*, who presented about 200 books to this library. But this library was sacked by *Bakhtiyar Khilji*. Sizable libraries were also established at other places like Jagaddoi, Mithila, Odantapuri etc.

Medieval period was predominated by Mughal regime. The birth of many other libraries of importance took place in this period. Buddhism and Jainism had their own school of philosophy. Karnataka was the center of Jainism. Many a time the book collection was a hobby of the kings there. Copying of manuscripts, translations and even the five building of books were persuaded with zeal. *Balban*, the eldest son of prince *Muhumud* had set up a library and his brother *Bhughra Khan* also had a library. They all loved books.

Khilji's laid down the foundation of maintaining the Imperial Library, where he also appointed a Librarian. A reference is also noteworthy to be made that *Shaikh Nizamud-din Auliya* also established a public library during this time. Besides, some other libraries housed in the education centers like *Madarsa, Maktab* and *Masjids* and the *Khanghas* also contained a good number of collections. Emperor *Babar's* Imperial Library was established in Delhi, which later shifted to Agra by his son *Humayun*. It had Indo-Muslim architecture style, billhead and rows of almirahs. Palu-leaf, birch-bark manuscripts formed the collection in this library.

Muslim saints did also play the role in furthering the cause of learning and the libraries like *Tabaqut-I-Nasiri, Ijaz-I-Kursrabi,* refer to places, which served as repositories for books. *Babu Fard-a-Sufi* saint and scholar (1173-1265 AD) had a library of standard works on religion and mysticism. Under slave dynasty, *Muhammed Gori* also established various libraries. Books were made available for consultation. During *Jalalu-ud-din* regime *Amir Khusro* was patronized and made keeper of the Holy Koran. The next dynasty was *Sayyad's* dynasty followed by Lodi's Dynasty. *Sultan Kikandar Lodi* was himself a poet and he established a library with a collection of many books. The *Sultan* of *Kashmir* also founded many libraries and educational institutes. The library of *Sultan* was known as Royal Library, and it was located with in his palace.

Hindu Kings – Royal Libraries

King *Bhoja of Dhara* established a Hindu Royal Library, which was shifted later to *Auhilvadpattan* by *Sidharaja*

Jaisuigadava after defeating the *Bhoja* in war. Later, it was merged with the Court Library of *Chalukyas*. There was a Royal Library in Raghunath temple, which housed the manuscripts. There was another library at Bikaner, which was well organized, preserved and maintained the stock in four figures.

The other libraries, which flourished well during the medieval time include:

(a) Saraswathi Mahal Library at Tanjore (Tamil Nadu)

(b) Bhaskaracharya Library at Patan (Gujarat)

(c) Kavindracharya Saraswati Library

(d) Jain Bhandars in Kathiawar (Gujarat)

(e) Masulipatam Library in Andhra Pradesh

(f) Fort St. George Library at Madras

(g) Fort St. David Library at Cuddalore

Bibliography

E. Allen and J. Seamen. Entering the Mainstream: The Quality and Extent of Online Education in the United States, 2003 (<http:/ www.sloan.c.org/resources/entering_ mainstream.pdf>)

Aho, Alfred and Sethi, Ravi. Compilers, principles, techniques and tools. Add Weslay. 2004

Akerman, Mark. "Augumenting the organizing memory: A field study of answer garden". Procg. ACM Conf. on computer supported coop. works (CSCW).

Allen, James F. "Towards conversational human computer interaction". Al Magazine. 22, 4, 2001.

Alexendria Digital Library Project. Alexendria Digital Library. Univ. of California, Santa Barbara (UCSB),

Website: http://Alexandria.sdc.uesb.edu.

ARL supplementary statistics. Association of Research Libraries. Website: www.arl.org.

Artstor. The Digital Library. Website: http://www.artstor.org.

Atkenson, Richard. "A new world of scholarly communications". Chronicle of higher education, Nov.7, 2003

Audio Engg. Society. Recommendations for Recorded Music Project Document AESTD 1002.1.03.10.

Website: www.aes.org./technical/document/AESTD1002.1.03. 10.1.pdf,2003

Bacon, Jean and Hayton, Richard. "Middleware for Digital Libraries." D-Lib Magazine. 1998.

http://www/dlib/org/dlib/october98/bacon/10bacon.html

Baguall. Digital imaging of Papyri. Commission on Preservation and Access. Washington: DC., Sept. 1995. ISBN 1-88734-44-0.

Baird, Henry S. "The skew angle of printed documents". Proceedings SPSE 40th Conf. on hybrid imaging system"., May 1987; pp.21.24.

Baldwin, Jerry. "Libraries reduce cost, add value". Technology Exchange Newsletter. Website: www.cts.umn.edu /T2/Tech Exch/2002/July-Sept/Library table.html,2002.

Berghel, Hal and O. German, Lawrence. "Protecting ownership rights through Digital water making". IEEE Computer. Vol. 29, No. 7, 1996; pp.101-103.

Bergman, Michael K. "The Deep web: Surfacing hidden value". J. of Electronic Publishing Aug. 2001. www.brightplanet.com/ deep content/tutorials/Deep web/ index.asp.

Berners-Lee, T. "World Wide Web: The Information Universe". Electronic Networking Research. Application Policy. Vol. 1, No. 2, 1992; pp.52-58.

Blair, David C. and Maron, M.E. "An evaluation of retrieval effectiveness for a fulltext document retrieval system". CACM.Vol.28, No. 3, 1985; pp.289-299.

Bloom, Floyd. "The rightness of copyright" Forbes. Vol. 131, 1983; p.196.

Bogart, John Van. Magnetic tap storage and handling: A guide for libraries and Archive commission on preservation and Access. Washington D.C. 1995.

Bolt, R.A. Spatial Data Management. Architecture Machine Group. Cambridge, 1979.

Borgman, Christine. "Why are online catalogs hard to use". J.Awe. soc. for Inf. Sc. Vol. 37, No. 6, 1986; pp.387-400.

Born, Gunter. The file formats handbook Van Nostrand Rienhold. N.4, 1995.

Borner, Katy. "Visualizing knowledge domains". Annual Review for Inf. Sc. & Tech. Vol. 37, 2003; pp.179-275.

Boursin, Francoise. "Stemming the flood of paper". Chemistry and Industry Magazine, 1995.

Brin, Surgey and Page, Lawrence. "The Anatomy of a long scale hypertextual web search engine". Computer networks and ISDN system. Vol. 30, 1998; p.107-112.

Broxis, P.F. "Syntactic and relationships: A review of Precis: A manual of concept analysis and subject indexing. D. Austin". Indexes, Vol. 10 No.2, 1976; pp.54-59.

Bripijalfsson, E. "the IT Productivity gap". Optimize No. 21, 2003.

Burrell, Quentin. "A not on aging in a library circulation model". J. Doc. Vol. 41, No.2, 1985; pp.100-115.

Carnevale, "Professors Seek Compensation for Online Courses," Chronicle of HigherEducation,August13,2004, <http://chronicle.com/free/v50/i49/49a02701.htm> (accessed November 4,2005).

Chepesink, Ronald. "JSTOR and electronic achieving". American Libraries. Vo. 31, No. 11, 2000; pp. 46-48.

Church, Ken. "A stochastic parts program and noun phrase purser for unrestricted text". 2nd Conference on applied natural language processing, ACL, 1988; pp.136-143.

Cloonan, Michde and Berger, Sid. "Present and future issues for special collections". Rare books and MSS Librarianship. Vol. 13, No.2, 1999; pp.89-94.

Consulting Trust GmbH, Strategic Study on New Opportunities for Publishers in the Information Services Market.

http://www2.echo.lu/impact/projects/studies/en/electrpub.html#reperel.

Cool, C. and Park, S. "Information seeking behaviour in new searching environment". COLIS 2, 1996; pp.239-160.

Croft, W.B. and Harding, S.M. "An evaluation of information retrieval accuracy with simulated OCR output". Sympasium on Document analysis and information retrieval. 1994; pp.115-126.

Cummings, Anthony M and Witte, Marcia, L. University library and scholarly communication Washington: Association of Research Libraries, 1992.

December, John. "Electronic Publishing on the Internet: New Traditions, New Choices". *Educational Technology,* 34 (7): pp. 32-36 (online)

(http://www.december.com/john/papers/et94.txt) 1994.

Dedrick, Jason and Vijay Gurlaxmi. "Information technology and economic performance. ACM computing survey. Vol. 35, No.1, 2003; pp. 1-28.

Dellit jillian,Eduaction (and EdNA) in the knowledge Age.

http://www.edna.edu.au/edna/go/engineName/filemanager/ped/337/99

Dempsey, Lorcan. "The Subject Gateway." Online Inf. Review. Vol. 24, no.1, 2000; 8.23.

Devine, J. Exploring what e-Learning is and is supposed to be, in e-learning europa life.

(http:www.elearningeuropa.onfe/docprint.pbp?id=1359&ing=1)

Drabenstott, K.M. and Burman, C.M. Analytical review of the library of the future. Council of Library Resources. Washington: DC, 1994.

Drucker, peter. Post Capital Society. Oxford: Butter worth-Heinemann, 1993.

Dumais, Sue. "Latent semantic analysis". Annual review of Information Science and Technology. Vol. 38, 2004; pp.189-230.

Egan, D.E. and Ramde, J.R. "Behavioural evaluation and analysis of a hypertext Browser". Procg. CHI89, 1989; pp.205-210.

Eklund, J. and Kay, K.E-learning: Emerging Issues and Key Trends (http://www/flexibllearning.net.au/research/2003/elearning250903final.pdf) 2004.

Eliot, Charles W. "The division of a library into books in use, and books not issue, with different storage methods for the two classes of books" Collection Management. Vol. 2, No.1, 1978; pp.73-82.

Ewalt, David. "Just how many Linux users are there". Information Week. June 2001.

Ewing, Jim and Miller, David. A framework for evaluating computer supported collaborative learning in Educational Technology & Society 5,1, 2002

(http://ifets.ieee.org/periodical1/vol_1_2002/ewing.html)

Fischer, Gerhard. "Symmetry of ignorance, Social Creativity, and Meta-design". Knowledge based systems. Vol.13, No.7,8, 2001.

Forsyth, David and Malik, Jitendra. "Finding pictures of objects in large collection of images". Object Representation in computer vision. Vol. 1144, 1996; p.335-360.

Fox, E and Lunin, L. "Perspectives on: Digital Libraries". Journal of the American Society for Information Sciences 44.

Fresko, Mac. Source of Digital Informations. Report 6102. London: British Library R&D Dept., 1994.

Garside, R. and Leech, G. The computational analysis of English. London: Longman, 1987.

Gibbs, W. Wayt. "Taking computers to task". Scientific American. 1997; pp.82-89.

Giberton, D. "Student-Recruitment Technique blasted by Feds: Univ. of Phoenix Audit leads to $9.8 mil Fina", the Arizona Republic. Sept. 14, 2004.

Gordon, Sallie and Gustavel, Jill. "The effect of hypertext on reader knowledge representation". Procgs of Human Factors Society-32 annual meeting. 1988; pp.296-306.

Gourley, Don. Opening Doors with Open Source. Computers in Libraries.

(http://www.infotaday.com/cilmag/oct00/gourley.htm)

Grunin, L. Electronic Publishing: Publish without Paper! *PC Magazine, 14(3)*, pp.110-119 [Online], 1995

http://rowlf.cc.wwu.edu:8080/~kenr/RevLitDox/elecpub.html#4

Guthrie, Kevin M. "Archiving in digital age: There is a will, there is a way". Education Review. Vol. 36, No.6, 2001; pp.56-65.

Hanptmann, Alexender G. and Jin, Rong. "video retrieval using speech and image information". Electronic imaging conference. Storage retrieval for multimedia databases, 2003.

Hawkins, Donald T. "Electronic books". Online. Vol. 26, 2002.

Hiltz, S.R. and Turoff, M. "The Evaluation of online Learning and the revolution in higher education". Communication of the ACD, Vol. 49,, No. 10, Oct. 2005; p.60.

Horn, Richard. The Network is the teacher: Collaborative e-learning Circuits ASTD's Online Magazine

(http://www. learningcircults.co,/jun2000/horn.html)

Howe-Steiger nd M.C Donohre," Faculty and Administration Collaborating for E-learning Courseware,"EDUCAUSE Quarterly, Vol 28, No.1, 2005,pp.20-32,

(<http:/www.edua=cause.edu/apps/eq/eqm05/eqm0513.asp>)

Humphray, Susanne. A knowledge based expert system for computer based assisted indexing". IEEE Expert Vol. 4, No.3, pp.25-38, 1989.

Jaimes, Alejandro and Chang, S.F. "Automatic selection of visual features and classifiers". Storage and retrieval for media databases, 2000.

Jonson, Michael. "Academic press gives away its secret of success". Chronicle of higher education. Vol.48, No.3, 2001; pp.24.

Jin, Rong. "Learning to identify video shots with people based on face detection". Procg. IEEE Int. & Conference on multimedia. Paper MD-PS. Battimore. 2003.

Jorgensen. Economic growth in the information age. Cambridge: MIT Press, 2002.

Karney, J. SGML and HTML: Tag Masters. PC Magazine, 14, 3, 1995; pp.144-171. Russell, Electronic Publishing, 1996.

Kiernan, K. "The Electronic Beowulf". Computers in Libraries. 1995; pp.14-19.

King Donald W. and Tenopir, Carol. "Scholarly journal and digital database pricing. PEAK Conference, 2000.

King, Donald W. and Tenopir, Carol. "Using and reading scholarly literature". Annual Review of Information Science and Technology Vol. 311, 2001; pp.423-477.

Knex, D. "Enhancing Accessibility of Lab Materials". SIGCSE Bulletin. 29, 4. 1997; pp.20-21.

Kleinberg, Jon. "Authoritative sources in a hyperlinked environment". J.ACM. Vol. 46, No.5, 1999; pp.604-632.

Lamel, Lori and Gauvain, Jean. "Automatic processing of broadcast audio in multiple language. XI Enro. Signal Conf. 2002 paper 702.

Lancaster, F.W. Towards Paperless Information System N.Y.: Academic Press, 1978.

Licklidar, J.C.R. The Future of Libraries: Cambridge MIT Press, 1965.

Lessig, Lawrence. The future of ideas. N.York: Random House, 2001.

Logoze, Carl and Fielding, David. Defining Collections in Distributed Digital Libraries. D-Lib Magazine, November 1998.

(http://www.dlib.org/dlib/november98/logoze/11lagoze.html)

Lyman, Peter and Varain, Hal "Howmuch Information 2003?". Website www.simsberkeley.edu/research/project/ how-much-info-2003/.

Mychup, F. The Production and Distribution of knowledge. N.J., Princeton Univ. Press, 1962.

Martinich, L. Future trends in e-learning: Lessions from history. (http://www.educationon.edu.on/globalmmit/papers/lmartinic.html).2004

McGovern, Gerry. "Quality publishing is about saying no.". Website: www.gerrymegovern.com/nt/2003/nt~2003.0804htm 2003.

Mekenny,Carol. Improving Teaching and Learning through the use of new technology.

http://www.edna.edu.au/edna/go/engineName/filemanager/pid/337/991001_improveteachlearnv1pdf?actionreq=actionfile Download&fid=12624>

Morris, R. "Scatter storage techniques". Comm. of ACM. Vol.11, 1988; pp.38-43.

Nielsen, Jakob. The Difference Between Web Design and GUI Design. Alertbox, 1 May 1997.

(http://www.useit.com/alertbox/9705a.html)

Nielsen, Jakob and Phillips. V.L. Information retrieval of in perfectly recognized handwriting.

Website: www.useit.com/papers/handwriting.retrieval.html, 1993.

"Numbers" Time Dec. 5, 2005. p. 29.

(http://www.Time.com/time/agazine/article/0,9171,1134786.00html>)

O'hara, Kenton and Smith, Fiona. "Student readers' use of library documents". Procg. ACMSIGEHI 1998; pp.233-240.

Okerson, Am and O' Donald, James. Rememberance of thing, past, present and future". Publisher's Weekly, Vol. 239; No.34, 1992; 22-29.

"Online Learning", Govt. of Technology, Vol. 18, Issue 9, Sept. 2005.

Pachnowski L.M. and J.P.Jurcyk. "Perceptions of Faculty on the Effect of Distance Learning Technology of Faculty Preparation Time," Online Journal of Distance Learning Administration, Vol.VI,No. III, fall 2003

<http://www. Westga.edudistance/ojdla/fall63/pachnowskis64.html>(accessed November 4,2005).

Peacocke, R.D. and Graft, D.H. "Introduction to speech and speaker recognition". IEEE Computer Vol. 23, No. 8, 1990; pp.26-33.

Pentland, Alex. "Smart Rooms". Scientific American. Vol. 274; No.4, 1996; pp.54-62.

Perrone, Michael P. and Russell, Gregor F. "Machine learning in a multimedia document retrieval framework". IBM system journal. Vol. 41, No.3, 2003; pp.494-503.

Potamianos, Gerasimos, Neti, Chalapthy. "Large-Vocabulary audio-visual speech recognition machine and humans". Procgs. EUROSPEECH, 2001.

Quinn L.M. and Corry, M. "Factors That Deter Faculty from Participating in Distance Education," Online Journal of Distance Learning Admisistratio,Vol.V,No.IV ,Winter 2002,

<http://www. Estga.edu/-distance/ojdla/winter54/Qiomm54.htm> 2005.

Ramsland, Katherine. The origin of voiceprint. Website:

(www.crimelibrary.com/criminal_mind/forenrics/voiceprints.html).2004.

Rensik, Philip and Yorousky, David. "Distinguishing systems and distiguishing senses: New evaluation methods for word sense disambiguation". Natural Language Engineering. Vol.5 No.2, 1999; pp.113-139.

Rider, Frement. The scholarmid the future of research library. N.York: Hatham Press, 1944.

Robertson, George and Czonwinski, Maly. "Data maintain: Using memory for document management". ACM sympasium. SanFrancisco. 1998; pp.153-162.

Rudever, Lawrence and Millar Whitehead, Marie. "Who is reading online education journal?" Why and what are they reading". D-Lib. Magazine. Vol. 8, No. 12, 2002.

Russel, T.L. The No significant Difference Phenomenon: A Comparative Research Annotated Bibliography on Technology for distance education. All: International D-Education Certification Centre, 1999.

Salton, G.A. and Buchley, C. "Automatic Processing of foreign language documents". Jrl. of Ame. Society for Inf. Sc. Vol. 21, No. 3, 1970; pp. 187-194.

Salton, G.A. and Buckley. "Automatic text structuring and retrieval: Experiments in automatic encyclopedia searching". Procg. INSIGIR Conf. 1991; pp. 21-30.

Samual, A.L. "the Banishment of paper work". New Scientist. Vol. 21, No. 380, 1964, pp.529-41.

Satoh, S. and Nakarmura, Y. "Name it: Naming and detecting faces in news videos. IEEE Forum: Vol. 24, No. 3, 1990; pp.62-75.

Schell, G.P. "Universities Marginalize Online Courses: Why Should Faculty Members Develop Online Courses If the Effort May Be Detrimental to their Promotion or Tenure?" Communications of the ACM, July 2004, pp. 53-56.

Scheuermann, B.M. Is the role of the teacher as the 'knowledge authority' in danger in the ICT-learning setting? In elearningeuropa.info.

http://www.elearninguropa.onfo/docPrint. php?id=580&Ing=1

Schifter, C.C. "Faculty participation in Asynchronous Learning Networks: A case Study of Motivating and Inhibiting factors," Journal of Asynchronous Learning Networks, Vol4,Issue, 4, June 2000<http:/www.sloanc.orf/publications/jaln/v4n1/pdf/v4n1_schifte4r.pdf> (accessed November 4,2005).

Shah, Urvi and Finin, Tini. "Information retrieval on the semantic web". 10th Inel Conf. on Inf. & Knowledge Management 2002.

Shardanand, Upendra and Maes, Pattle. "Social information filtering: Algorithms for automating word of mouth". Prg. CHI Conf. on human factors in computing system. 1995; pp.210-227.

Shneiderman, Ben. "User interface design and evaluation for an electronic encyclopedia". Cogn. Engg. In Design.... Expert system. Vol.5, No.4, 1978; pp.417-439.

Shneiderman, Ben. "Tree visualization with tree maps". ACM transaction on graphics. Vol.11, No.1, 1992; pp.92-99.

Spark-Jonee, Karen. "Languae and Information, old idea, new achievement". Website: www.cl.com.ac.uk/users/ksj/GH lect 02.pdf (http://la.cs.cmu.edu./callen), 2002.

Strayer Education, Washington post, October 28,2005, p.D04, <http://www. Washingtonpost.Com/wpdyn/content/article/ 2005/10/27/Ar2005102702226.html> (Accessed November 14,2005)

Swanson, Don R. and Smalheiser, N.R. "An interactive system for finding supplementary literature". Artificial intelligence. Vol. 91, No.2, 1997.

Swanson, Don R. and Smalheiser, N.R. "Information discovery from complementary literature". Jrl. Am. Soc. for Inf. Sc. and Tech. Vol. 52, No. 10, 2001; pp.797-812.

Twigg, C.A. Innovations in Online Learning :Moving Beyond No Significant Difference, The Pew Learning and Technology Program Center For Academic Transformation at Rensselaer Polytechnic Institute, 2001 p. 23,< hppt://www. Center.rpi.edu/Pewsum/Mono4.phf>(accessed November 4, 2005)

U.S. News & World /Report , E-Learning Guide, Business Degrees Online,Accred-ite Programs, <http://www. Usnews.com/usnews/edu/elearning/tables/mba_reg.htm> (accessed November 4, 2005).

Varis, T. New literacies and e-learning compentencies, iln elearning europa.info.

Wactlar, Howard. Informedia Digital Video Library

Website: http://www.informedia.cs.cmu/edu.

Walker, Thomas. "Market-driven fuel access to journal articles". The Scientist. Vol. 15, No. 12, 2001; p.43-7.

Wilson, J.M. "Adventures in Education: The Maintenance Contract for Lifetime Education Association, March 30, 2005, slides 6 and 7,

<http://www.jackmwilson.com/ArticlesTalks/UCEAMarch2005.ppt>(accessed November 4, 2005).

Waltham, Mary. Who do publication cost so much?

Website: www.marywaltham.com/denver_SLA.app) 2002.

OTT